Discernment and Commitment

On the Making of Europe

From Horatio we received the old saying 'tua res agitur', it is your concern! Yet Horatio added something: 'paries cum proximus ardet', when your neighbour's house is on fire. Exactly for this reason we are all responsible for Europe, as if it is burning.
This series reflects on issues related to the shaping of Europe.

If you would like to join in the debate, if you have questions or suggestions, please write to Prof. Dr. Jurjen Wiersma. Titiaanstraat 52, B-1040 Brussels, Belgium.

1. Discernment and Commitment, Kampen, 1993.

Discernment and Commitment

Bruno Ackermann
Harry M. de Lange
Duncan B. Forrester
Daphne Hampson
Jan Niessen
Ignacio Ramonet
Peter Sedgwick
Maartje van Putten
Jurjen Wiersma (ed.)

Kok Pharos Publishing House
Kampen – the Netherlands

CIP-GEGEVENS KONINKLIJKE BIBLIOTHEEK, DEN HAAG

Discernment

Discernment and commitment / Bruno Ackermann... [et al.; ill.: Alies Wiersma]. – Kampen: Kok Pharos. – Ill. – (On the making of Europe; nr. 1)
ISBN 90-390-0022-0
NUGI 631/661
Trefw.: politieke theologie.

P.O. Box 130, 8260 AC Kampen, the Netherlands
Cover Design By Rob Lucas
Typesetting: Elgraphic bv, Schiedam
ISBN 90 390 0022 0
NUGI 631/661

Series on Europe

Contents

1. Introduction

JURJEN WIERSMA

World War II is finished. The Cold War is also said to be over. Yet these days see horrible events reach a frightening zenith in the former Republic of Yugoslavia. Although this awful tragedy does not immediately affect any of the twelve Member States of the European Community, obviously the Yugoslav implosion may turn into an explosion capable of setting other regions of Europe aflame. So far the hostilities have been limited in character, but the next time this Balkan fire may easily ignite other parts of the European continent. What makes marshal Tito's originally hopeful federation of brave partisanship particularly threatening is its extreme militarisation. But, to put it in Machiavellian terms, there is no prince, who might forge together the various bands of competitive citizen-soldiers or combate the current policy of corruption and disruption. There are merely the vicissitudes of fortune and fate, i.e. fortuna and necessità, that undermine any kind of public order in certain sections of Europe.

Can we cope with the existing (dis)order in Europe? As far as Europe at large is concerned there is apparently neither a dominating prince nor an oddering principle to facilitate a humane habitat where peace, justice and friendship might find a prosperous shelter. As a matter of fact princes and principles probably constitute the minor question in a Europe in full process of reconstruction today. The major question is without any doubt its citizenry. As the British-German sociologist and politician Ralph Dahrendorf once said: Civil society is the key. The Italians, in turn, would say that the articulation of *vivere civile* is the key issue. In this they are right, Dahrendorf would stress, adding that in order to produce a civil society men and women should be civilian. This idea was referred to in East Central Europe during the perestroika period of the former Soviet President Gorbachev. The concept of civil society should be fashionable throughout Europe. It is true, people should be civilian: 'that is, polite, tolerant and above all, non-violent'.[1]

In the same vein it may be argued that human beings should advocate de-militarisation. That is to say, the organisation of our continent, which, it is often maintained, was accelerated by Hitler's hordes and swords, can only be advanced provided Europeans no longer fight each other in one way or another, but act and talk together for better for worse. To put it differently, in Europe we should give up any Machiavellian policies and turn to Grotian precepts. Both Nicollò Machiavelli and Hugo Grotius can be considered the representatives of a statesmanship which aims at unifying frantic factions, disruptive regions and predatory individuals, Whereas Machiavelli appealed to the assistance of citizen-soldiers. Grotius on the other hand, in attempting to bring about some sort of a unified and peace-filled commonwealth, proved himself a thoughtful and intelligent protagonist of a religious, political and social ecumene avant la lettre. For that reason, consciously adapting means to ends, Grotius sought support from among quite a different category, let us call this: citizen-civilians.

Hugo de Groot or Hugo Grotius (1583-1645) in his magnum opus *De Iure Belli ac Pacis* stresses two main concepts.[2]
These concepts must be considered inextricably intertwined. On the one hand, the widely renowned Dutch scholar and jurist, embarking upon an old Stoic wisdom, held that one of

the most striking anthropological features is humankind's sense of community. According to Grotius humankind has its roots in a primordial propensity, i.e. an *appetitus societatis*. In this basic human characteristic Grotius found the layer that he thought solid enough to function as an anchor for global human society. In other words, the Dutchman founded and fostered international law as natural law, emphatically stressing that, whereas the laws of each separate state bear the interests of that state in mind, a good number of laws might originate as common to all states, or a great many states. In the latter case, it is evident that the laws bear in mind, the interests, not of specific states, but of the wider society of states, the so-called *magna humana societas*.

On the other hand, Grotius affirms that nature has put an awareness of and a desire for justice, peace and conviviality in all human beings. In his view, individual conscience plays a pre-eminent role, in particular with regard to the military duty to obey. Deviating from Roman, Germanic and Scholastic standards of law, and thus deviating from the principle of 'respondeat superior', which discharged the subordinate from personal responsibility, Grotius, in *De Iure* stresses the subordinate's right and duty to disobey unjust orders. In other words, he rejects the instrumentalist position of subordinates. They are not to be dealt with as an instrument in the hands of a superior, be it a State or a Sovereign. One must make one's own choices and decisions, as if God does not exist and as if one can only resort to one's own conscience. This emphasis on conscience in *De Iure*, leads Grotius to attribute a fair degree of individual responsibility to subordinates, for example soldiers. The idea of subordinates as instruments in the hands of superiors is totally absent. There is no presumption of the legality of orders, neither is there a claim on the self-evident conformity of positive human law with higher divine law.

In the case of war or illegitimate acts directed towards non-belligerent persons, to note just the worst of a wide variety of potential violations of a human being's integrity, the subjects are supposed to enquire into the (in)justice of the causes of war. They ought to decide themselves and Grotius believed them capable of doing so. Men are equipped with a conscience, are they not? That autonomous moral force happens to induce them to respectable choices and responsible actions.[3]
Unfortunately, Grotius' extraordinary appetite is not the sole drive at work in Europe in the last decades of the twentieth century. Although the first half of this century came to acknowledge that the creation of the world through a strategy of a national-socialist, chauvinist, populist or nationalist nature resulted in a complete fiasco, once again anti-societal forces are beating the big drum, perpetrating a great many evil deeds and even crimes against humanity. Without any exaggeration and not without a sense of anxiety, we may come to the conclusion, as we look at the current socio-political scene in Europe, that today civil society is in jeopardy. Moreover, from a Christian point of view, we may conclude that, in addition to an anti-Grotian appetite for political destruction and social distortion, an overt lust for a new heathendom is infiltrating the human arena. For example in Flanders, since 1991 'het Vlaams Blok' (the Flemish Bloc) all of a sudden came to the political forefront, successfully recruiting a fresh constituency on the basis of a rather appealing (and appalling) slogan, that says: 'Our people first'. One step further, and Flanders will witness its own kind of ethnic cleansing. Obviously people, who are, in general, profoundly secularised and by implication have lost the memory of the Gospel, are no longer in touch with its core message. That message is straightforward: God has aligned Himself with one single people, i.e. the people of the Convenant. In an equally straightforward manner the Gospel denounces any

distinction between a would be sanguine inner circle of intimi and a corrupt outer circle of aliens. In this context Paul, writing to the Galatians and convinced that he was bringing the good news of justice and at-one-ment, reminds us of he new order brought about by Christ, and which is still calling us to bring it to fulfilment:
'There can be neither Jew nor Greek, there can be neither bond nor free, there can be no male and female. For ye all are one human being in Christ Jesus'.

In one way or an other many people of good will follow a similar path, not with the intention of imitating Christ but merely because they are equipped with some kind of wider conscience that tells them to gather as many building-stones as possible for the erection of a solid European House, that, in turn, may be considered a corner-stone of Grotius' project of an encompassing commonwealth. Perhaps all men and women who are in favour of such a project already constitute an emerging partnership, an ecumene of enlightened and civil people. As far as Europe is concerned, the Treaty of Rome (1957) that established the European Economic Community (EEC) is certainly an essential milestone on the slippery route towards equality and unity on a traditionally fear- and war-ridden continent. But, as we indicated above, other forces are at work and we can identify disparate tendencies in Europe. On the one hand we are apparently on the track, on the other hand we are certainly on the wrong track. Europe is a continent of hope and promise but it is also a continent of despair and disillusion. In short, Europe is an ambivalent entity; ambiguity is its hallmark. Anti-European forces and pro-European forces are keen to profile themselves, attempting to win a large degree of influence and legitimacy.

All this makes Europe into a historical site beset with hitherto unknown critical junctures. It is appropriate for human beings, or rather it is a very human characteristic, to ask questions at the critical junctures in their history. That is exactly what is being done and will be done by a great number of contributors to a series of booklets 'on the making of Europe' of which this is the first volume. In it the authors try to discern what is happening in Europe. It is their hope that these observations will be of a transcending nature so that people may feel urged to leave behind the perplexities and complexities in which they are often caught and, instead, commit themselves to the shaping of a just and peaceful Europe.

The European phenomenon is approached from various angles, although one realises apriori that, given the very many dilemmas to be faced, the matter cannot be dealt with exhaustively in one small publication. Yet it is urgent and cogent for men and women to become involved in European affairs. Standing aloof or staying neutral is no longer permissable. That is the conviction the contributors to this volume have in common; they agree on the need for people, albeit as a matter of trial and error, to care about Europe, its future and its survival, and indeed that of the world in general. As Hannah Arendt suggested, the organisation of a people (in Europe) arises from their acting and speaking together. The articles included here may be said to have been composed in line with this challenging moral imperative. The material can and will perhaps, we hope, arouse some enthusiasm amongst readers, aiding them to explore the route towards a united and conscientious Europe.[4]

As Ignacio Ramonet's text demonstrates the essays contained in this volume may be seen against the overarching background of a whole world that finds itself in a global process of reconstruction. The years of construction and, in particular, the epoch of baffling techno-industrial expansion have gone. The Faustian and Promethean standards have for decades fascinated the human mind, now they seem to have reached their limits. Science, technology and economics clearly are not the unconditional vehicles of salvation which the academic establishment once claimed them to be. Even public opinion is of the conviction that first and foremost profound changes are required in the Western hemisphere. The Faustian threshold has been attained but humankind cannot be said to have amassed a maximum of happiness or an optimum of hope. On the contrary, it is caught up in a vicious circle of waste and want, of divergence and dismay, of confusion and contrition. Can we find a way out of this dreary threadmill, Ramonet wonders. Whatever the response to this question and to the root problems we must face today, the French political commentator confronts us with the ultimate question: Are we prepared to reconstruct the world, Europe included, totaliter aliter, totally otherwise – e.g. in terms of an unremitting human rights perspective?

After this initial bird's eye view the contributions which follow go into detail, mapping out what it means to come to grips with the (re)making of Europe. On the eve of the EC Edinburgh Summit it was William Pfaff who, in *The Herald Tribune* of November 26, 1992, and astonished at Europe's current fragility, touched upon the anti-European forces which have been set in operation. In his opinion, it is Prime Minister John Major (and, we must add, it was Prime Minister Margaret Thatcher) who has displayed a total inability to contain anti-European forces within his governing Conservative Party. Moreover, Pfaff blamed the public and the press for distancing Britain from European cooperation more than ever. In comparison with Pfaff's somber diagnosis this volume, with three outstanding papers from Britain, sounds quite a different note from the UK. Although Hampson, Forrester and Sedgwick do not mobilise uncompromisingly pro-

European forces, they quite explicitly have no wish to stand aloof. All three offer promising prospects of the new world they expect Europe to become some day. Hampson, writing as a feminist, a theologian and a human being, although suspicious of Europe, refers to the traditional sense of openness, diversity, and democracy so characteristic of Britain. She contends that this typical British legacy cannot be missed in Europe. Next to the old she attributes a significant momentum to the new, i.e. a synthetic feminist spirituality.

Forrester, in turn, focuses attention upon the 'place' of the Church and of Church theology in the Europe of the future. In the widely ranging landscape of old and new ecclesiastical stances he makes a serious effort to chart an alternative path between a triumphalist and a marginalist position. Rejecting these two options, Forrester appeals for an updating of the ecclesio-christological adage *ubi Christus ibi ecclesia* (where Christ is, there is the Church). To put it in other words: The broader 'Church' is to be found in the commitment to those with whom Christ used to identify, the poor, the weak and the oppressed. Sedgwick, finally, has taken the delicate relation between Church and State as a theme to ponder, and, more specifically, focuses on the triptych of national sovereignty, nation building and Church innovative influence. In the supernational Europe coming into being in the 1990s, in the midst of suffering and labour pains, the Churches must time and again safeguard the acknowledged values such as justice and freedom. What is needed, maintains Sedgwick, is an attitude of allegiance and loyalty towards the new Europe and of openness to the world, especially those who are vulnerable.

These qualities are unreservedly supported bij Ackermann in his exposé in which he describes the personalist outlook of Denis de Rougemont. The present chairman of the European Commission, the Frenchman Jacques Delors, is believed himself to be a personalist with regard to his world view and his idea of man. This being the case, it in intriguing to listen to Mr Delors addressing an audience at the Royal Institute of International Affairs in London on September 7, 1992. Speaking on the New European Order and the New World Order he used a peculiar metaphor: 'The contribution that the Community as such can make to the New World Order can, to use an image from the plant world, be considered something of a hybrid, what is produced by crossing a world power with an international organisation. I have been struck by the gradual emergence of the Community in this dual role on the international stage'. Something of a hybrid! What phenomenon is this? Is it not something that reminds us of the Promethean and Faustian presumptuousness which fails to acknowledge human limitations and, equally, loses sight of the human scale? That is why Ackermann's article is of major interest. In it light is shed upon an alternative potentiality – a personalism of human dimensions – for a world that, rightly or wrongly, has been labelled as a hybrid by a European architect, who without a doubt captures many ears and who, in his capacity of an opinion-maker in political affairs, needs to be able to look to sincere ideological critique and contrasting concepts.

It is in this vein that the three Dutch contributions are conceptualised, having in common a series of contrasting devices, all of which aim to give voice to the large number of marginalised people inside and outside Europe. De Lange, drawing upon the vast number of inspiring sources that have flowed from the Ecu-Movement into the wilderness of the modern world, raises the question of whether or not political power can be transferred to 'Brussels', in order to tame and to control it. It is precisely here that he sees the gateway which will allow the Churches to come in and deploy a counterbalancing force. De Lange reminds us of the Churches'

vocation to constitute a movement of resistance against fatalism, first and foremost economic fatalism. The market place is certainly not the exclusive site where human beings are supposed to look for their prosperity, health, and wealth. Van Putten has an eye for the predicament of the Indians, who in her opinion are pars pro toto representing the countless people at the margin of the planetary scene, in the centre of which Europe demonstrates a notable will for self-reliance and self-assertion. The survival of these people is at stake, according to Van Putten. She believes that Europe's democratic potential eventually must turn the scales. Niessen is of the same conviction, insisting that Europe, in order to be or not to be, should profile itself as a participatory society. He offers a sober inventory of the plight of migrants, refugees, and minorities on our continent, sensitising us to the intermediary role the so-called non-governmental organisations might assume in establishing a participatory democracy in a Europa about to be born.
Niessen's description of the real and objective facts is less alarming than we are usually prepared to believe, whilst his prescription of what ought to be done is more challenging than, on the average, we are willing to bring about: a new Europe harbouring a participatory and democratic landscape where it is very pleasant for people, young and old, migrants and foreigners, black and white, to dwell and to settle. Last but not least, an artist makes an incisive effort to come to terms with the emerging Europe, struggling to become a new creation, abounding in civility, peace, justice, honesty, and, above all, non-violence and tolerance. Alies Wiersma offers a couple of personal impressions that fills us with a sincere hope that, for Europe, the best is yet to be.
That is, in short, *vivere civile*!

Notes

1. Ralph Dahrendorf. *Reflections on the Revolution in Europe*. London, 1990. 93-94.
2. Hugonis Grotii. *De Iure Belli ac Pacis, libri tres*. P.C. Molhuysen (ed.) and C. van Vollenhoven (preface). Lugdunum Batavorum (=Leyden), 1919. See *Prolegomena*: 'Inter haec autem quae homini sunt propria, est appetitus societatis'.
3. B.P. Vermeulen. *Grotius on Conscience and Military Orders*. In: *Grotiana, new series VI*, 1985.
4. Hannah Arendt. *The Human Condition*. Chicago and London, 1973. 198-200. Cf. Hannah Arendt. *Eichmann in Jerusalem. A report on the banality of evil*. New York, 1976. 103-104. '...conscience as such had apparently got lost in Germany...'.

2. The New Order, Rebellion, Nationalism

Rebuilding the world*

IGNACIO RAMONET

It is an incredible paradox: at the very time the Universal Exhibition in Seville, with all its faith in the future, opens its doors, a kind of world-wide sinistrosis[1] is spreading in a climate of generalised grousing and disenchantment; it is clear to everyone that the only certainty is uncertainty. Following the collapse of the communist regimes in the East and the implosion of the Soviet Union – the major aims which the West has stubbornly pursued for decades – the climate should have been one of euphoria and triumph. It isn't. Quite unexpectedly, this victory has resulted in a malaise: '*We are confronted by a world which is even more mysterious than the one that went before*',[2] admits Mr Robert Graves, the director of the CIA. Indeed, the conjunction of the crises is such, that there is the fear of a general worsening of tension, while we see the spread of Western arrogance, technical barbarism and a whole series of archaisms, and various forms of racism, hatred and xenophobia. The world has once again become a maze, and a new labyrinth of Daedalus.

How did we get to such a point? In the most diverse fields the upheavals of recent years have brought societies to the threshold of a fundamental splitting of the ways. The depth of certain political changes – German unification, the collapse of the USSR, the crisis within the United Nations, the abolition of Apartheid, the end of the conflicts in Angola, El Salvador, Cambodia and Afghanistan, the changes in Nicaragua, Ethiopia, Algeria and in Chile – have brought radical changes to the geo-strategic face of the earth. Other events, such as the construction of Europe, albeit at a slower pace, have also had a decisive influence on the ebb and flow of world political life, leading to a veritable cascade of upheavals.

This exceptional period corresponds to a real change in the times; and this has aroused new anxieties in the West, and a widespread malaise within developed societies. To such an extent that the leaders can offer no clear vision of the future. No one is capable of saying what the new age will be like. *'We are,'* says Alexander King, a co-founder of the Club of Rome, *'in the midst of a long and difficult process leading to the emergence, in one form or another, of a global society, the probable structure of which we still cannot imagine'.*[3]

The age of the heroes is at an end; we know today that everything is in solidarity and yet, at the same time, everything is in conflict. We know that the new order will encompass everything and that nothing will be excluded from its sphere of influence: politics, the economy, social affairs, culture and ecology. It is a sphere which is far too vast for the hegemonic ambitions of the United States, even after their crushing military victory in the Gulf War. *'The United States' position is paradoxical,'* admits Arthur Schlesinger, a former adviser to president Kennedy, *'it is a military superpower which cannot meet the costs of its own wars. It can have no great future as a superpower. It is not capable of governing the world'.*[4]

Moreover, as opposed to the aim of world unification under the guidance of Washington we see the vigorous revival of all sorts of national, religious and ethnic particularisms... A whole series of historic forces, which for long were frozen by the balance of terror, and which, today, are exploding in this stormy end to the century.

In this new context there is one fundamental concept which would seem to be in a state of serious confusion: that of the adversary, of the enemy, the threat, the danger. What is the dominant danger? Who is behind it? These questions, to which, for the last seventy years, the West always responded: *'communism', 'the USSR'*, henceforth go unanswered. Yet for any political regime such answers are basic and provide a structure. They condition the definition of a security system capable of preserving it and forestalling crises. Above all they enable it to build up a language with regard to its own identity. But the 'principal enemy' is no longer unequivocal; henceforward it is a monster of a thousand faces which, in turn, can take the form of the population time-bomb, drugs, nuclear proliferation, ethnic fanaticisms, AIDS, Islamic fundamentalism, the greenhouse effect, the radio-active cloud, etc. All of them threats which know no frontiers and are planetary in their dimension.

No longer ballasted by the weight of the two superpowers, the world is searching for a new stability and seems to be shaken by two powerful and contradictory phenomena. On the one hand, some states are seeking to ally and unite themselves with others with the aim of creating blocs – principally economic blocs – which are bigger, more solid and less vulnerable. Following the lead of the European Community – a political objective hitherto unknown – other groups of countries in North and South America, in North Africa, in Asia and in Eastern Europe are increasing the number of free-trade agreements, doing away with customs barriers and at the same time strengthening political alliances.

Opposing these associative movements we find multinational blocs which are being subjected to centrifugal forces and to convulsion (India, Sri Lanka, China, Czechoslovakia), others fall apart (Ethiopia, Somalia) or implode as they fragment (the Soviet Union, Yugoslavia) before the very eyes of their horror-stricken neighbours.

Some see the shock of these fusions and fissions as the major confrontation of the decade. According to Edgar Morin, for example: *'The key problem in the coming years will be the multi-faceted struggle between, on the one hand, the forces of association, confederation and federation, not only in Europe but throughout the world, and the forces of disunity, collapse, rupture, and conflict'.*[5]

These *'forces of disunity'* would seem to be stimulated by the rebirth of the ethnic concept of the nation-state. The romantic and anti-republican notion that the state should exercise its authority over an ethnically homogeneous community (one language, one religion), brought together within historic frontiers, divides ordinary people and splits societies. Such a concept raises anew the problem of minorities and of their rights. At the same time it encourages the irredentist claims such as, for example, those of Serbia which, after the war with Croatia and under the very nose of the UN peace-keeping force, is setting out to absorb those Serb-inhabitated regions of Bosnia-Herzegovina. Likewise, in the Caucasus, Armenia is still tempted to annex Upper-Karabakh, and Russia has its eyes on the Crimea.

This concept of nationalism,[6] which tore apart the Old Continent from the 19th century right up until the end of the First World War, is also reappearing in Western Europe thanks, strangely enough, to the construction of Europe. The latter has erased the contours of the nation-state, which increasingly feels ill at ease, trapped as it is between the European super-state, to which it finds itself constantly transferring powers and competences, and the various region-states to which, in the name of decentralisation, it is also being forced to hand over an even larger share of its prerogatives.

In the case of many of these region-states, the more they possess distinct cultural – and notably linguistic – characteristics, the more they affirm their political identity; this is true, for example, of the Flanders, Catalonia, the Basque country, Corsica, Lombardy. In some of these regions the most radical of nationalist movements look to far-left ideas for support (Basque country, Corsica, Northern Ireland); in others to a far-right ideology (Flanders, Lombardy), but all extol, and with the same passion, the mythical *'values of the original ethnic community'*.

Under such conditions, what will become of national sovereignty? It would seem to be being nibbled away on all sides. In the first place – and in such basic areas as currency, defence and foreign policy – by the obligations imposed by monetary agreements (membership of the European Monetary System, the International Monetary Fund, the Group of Seven...), military alliances (NATO...), and international treaties. But it is also being eaten away by more insidious factors arising from purely technical considerations. *'In a world in which everything is based on technology,'* says a former Director General of Scientific Affairs at the OECD, *'a great many agreements had to be reached on very specific matters to enable the international system to function, be it with regard to the allocation of radio frequencies and air routes, security regulations, the standardisation of industrial components, etc. In each case, this brought about an imperceptible limitation of national freedom of action, the cumulative effect of which is far from negligeable.'*[7]

This dissolution of the identity of the State has served to intensify political confusion, particularly in Western Europe as we have seen recently in the elections in Belgium, Austria, France, Germany, Italy and the United Kingdom... In all countries the political class appears to be discredited, the dominant parties inspire little confidence and are losing voters. In the United States, with only a few months to go to the presidential election, 75% of Americans are *'not satisfied'* with the candidates, Bush and Clinton. In Japan we see a similar phenomenon. Preparation for next July's elections to the Senate is going ahead in an atmosphere of political disarray; the government and the Liberal Democratic Party (LDP) in power are divided and are not respected. Pessimism is rife.

Parties and political leaders are held responsible for the crisis within a society which offers neither security nor solidarity and in which all sorts of frustrations are on the increase. Ordinary people are, apparently, fed up with bad management, with corruption, the way public services fail to work, with insecurity, the lack of reform, excessive bureaucracy and the lack of concern on the part of the State. Andre Gorz comments: *'Given this society, a society which has become a stranger to itself, we find, in every country, two types of rebellion. On the one hand, those people who, culturally, are equipped to handle their own autonomy call for the creation and preservation of a new, self-managed form of socialisation and self-determined activities, against the power of the State and the power of money. On the other we have the regressive reaction of those who would like to return to the security offered by a pre-modern, stable hierarchical order, one highly conducive to integration, in which, from birth, each individual has his appointed place assigned to him by his membership of a given nation or race.'*[8]

These new forms of rebellions have taken over from the revolts of the labour movement, inspired by a specific vision of the future, which also disappeared with the collapse of the communist regimes. Moreover, society no longer sees itself in terms of social classes. But how, in political terms, can we express conflicts which are no longer class conflicts?[9] *'The end of class politics, and perhaps even of the classes themselves,'* writes the sociologist Ralf Dahrendorf, *'means that there is no natural electorate for a programme of reform. The countries of the OECD are dominated by a majority class representing 60%, 70% or 80% of electors who, as a whole, believe that their aspirations will be fulfilled if things continue more or less as they are. They do not call for any major reforms; indeed, on the contrary, all they want is security, a bit of luck, a government which fills their pockets, and bank accounts which always pay interest.'*[10]

If there is no *'natural electorate for a programme of reforms'* (which the new socialist government in France would seem to admit, as it suspends, one by one, all the planned reforms) what will become of the left? What will become of socialism? Mr Lionel Jospin, First Secretary of the French Socialist Party from 1981 to 1988, is quite blunt. *'There is little reason to believe that socialism, as a specific mode of production, has any future.'*[11] Thus, as we see, this identity crisis affects the principal role players in political life.

Yet despite this sense of stupor afflicting the left, liberalism does not appear to enjoy mass support among the electors. Rigorously applied during the 1980s in the United States by Mr Reagan and by Mrs Thatcher in the United Kingdom, this economic and political doctrine has brought with it very painful social consequences. It has worsened inequalities, increased unemployment, led to the decline of industrialisation, a decline in public services, the decay of collective institutions... According to the prophets of monetarism all these problems would automatically be solved by economic expansion. The greatest experts were of the opinion that, thanks to deregulation and 'the globalisation of the financial market', shortfalls would be systematically financed by profits, and expansion would become perpetual... Before our eyes we see the broken debris of all these unfulfilled promises.

This easy creation of wealth was encouraged even in countries with socialist governments, such as Spain and France. And the new rich, sometimes captains of industry, were held up by government and the media as models to be imitated, the symbols of society's reconciliation with capital. Financial speculation was encouraged. The apotheosis of the 'golden boys' was cause for celebration.

With the crash of 1987 and the bursting of the financial bubble bankruptcies followed the one upon the other, and led to the discoveries of the incredible swindles typical of the casino economy. In Japan, for example, on the list of the ten largest fortunes published in the monthly *Nikkei Venture* we find only three millionaires who owe their wealth to activities relevant to the real economy. The seven others are speculators.

Many of those who, in the course of the second half of the 1980s, were held up as models because of their lightning rise to riches are today charged with fraud, extortion, misconduct and other crimes. Many are in prison. The heroes of neo-liberalism are tricksters. The list is impressive: from Robert Maxwell to Donald Trump; from Alan Bond, the Australian millionaire, to Michael Milken, the inventor of junk bonds; from Ivan Boesky, the Wall Street wizard, to Nui Onoué, the female advisor of the Kabuto-chọ; from Giancarlo Parretti to Claude Bez and to Carlo De Benedetti. More specifically, this concept of the Monopoly economy is directly responsible for the problems facing the American savings and loan funds (which lost 400 thousand million dollars) and the ruin of many small savers.[12] It proves, yet again, the fallacious presuppositions of ultracapitalism which Galbraith, with caustic irony, described as follows: *'The bulk of capital is, of necessity, in the hands of people endowed with exceptional intellectual power.'*[13] Capitalism, which emerged the victor over Stalinist socialism, thus, itself, is discredited... and indeed to such an extent that in the United States and England in particular there is growing nostalgia for the welfare-state dismantled in the name of market forces. Many people condemn the trap of the dual society with, on the one hand, a group of people who are hyperactive and, on the other, the vast mass of those whose jobs are precarious, the unemployed and the underclass.

This two-speed society does not scandalise everyone. To quote Mr Bernard Tapie, the former French Minister for Urban Affairs: *'It is neither conceivable nor serious to think of providing a job, or at least a productive job, for everyone. We made a mistake in trying to prevent any increase in the number of the unemployed'.*[14]

We were to prevent it even less as the economic recession worsened and affected not only the United States but also Canada, Australia and England, not to mention the countries of Eastern Europe and those of the former USSR. Even Germany and Japan, once considered safe, have gradually been affected. The eastern part of Germany has gone through a veritable 'social crash'; while, for its part, the Japanese stock exchange, in 1992, experienced a sort of slow-motion crash, with a fall of 40% (it had already seen a fall of 38.7% in 1990) which shows no sign of stopping.

No salvation outside the market?

Despite all these disappointments, the neo-liberal model continues to expand. In the South it has been imposed by the major financial organisations such as the World Bank and the International Monetary Fund. Macro-economic indicators – inflation, currency, budgetary deficits, foreign trade, growth – are set up as absolute imperatives to which everything else must be sacrificed, while economies are subjected to energetic plans of structural adjustment so that they can integrate into the international market. This is the only way to salvation, or so it is claimed. Jean-François Revel states, for example, that *'Only the coupling of democracy and the market can offer any way out for both communism and underdevelopment'.*[15] An opinion ratified by one of the leading gurus of neo-liberalism, the American economist Jeffrey Sachs: *'It is my deep conviction that the key to solving many problems, including the problem of development, lies in integration into the world economy'.*[16]

The idea is spreading – and this the right-wing has never ceased to say since the outset – that there is one way and one way only to conduct a country's economic affairs; and that all economies are, henceforward, inter-linked. This economism has established a new form of totalitarianism, with its own dogmas and its own high priests. In the name of the 'total market' this new ideology is gradually taking over both the planet and all human activities. It is the market which dictates what is true, beautiful, good and right. 'Market laws' have become the new Tablets of the Law which must be revered; they are defined by the famous 'invisible hand' which, in its infinite wisdom, regulates and orders all transactions within an interdependent world. To depart from these laws is to take the road to ruin and to decay.

Thus, in Eastern European Countries in particular, these laws are applied with all the fanaticism of the newly converted... despite all the social costs and despite the protests of people such as Mikhail Gorbatchev: *'that 80% of the Russian people live below the poverty level and that we neglect the poorest of the poor and think only of macro-economic stabilisation is something quite intolerable'.*[17]

Once upon a time, economists in the East proclaimed: *'Anything which fails to obey the Plan must be condemned'.* These same economists, now converted to liberalism, today affirm, with equal conviction: *'Anything which fails to obey market laws must be condemned'.*

These laws based on competition and competitiveness call for a spirit of combat and permanent rivalry; they encourage production at the lowest possible cost. Since, in recent years, technological progress has indeed stimulated productivity, it is possible to produce more in less time, and with lower wage costs. In France, the annual period of work has decreased by a third over a period of thirty years, yet output has doubled. If we can create ever more wealth without creating jobs, then unemployment will become endemic, unless we agree, like the Greens, to job-sharing.

Otherwise, in the name of balance, companies will continue to lay people off. In the context of the end of the Cold War, the American arms industry alone plans to do away with some 500,000 jobs between now and 1995. In the United Kingdom, in the same sector, there will be 40,000 job losses. In France, 18,000 jobs will be lost this year, and in this industry some 100,000 jobs will disappear by 1995 (a quarter of all jobs)...

In the South the blind application of these same laws has led to situations of tension; theoretically at least, the countries become richer (if we are to believe the macro-economic indicators), whereas the local people become poorer. Recently in Venezuela this led to social unrest and an attempted military coup... In Peru, President Fujimori forestalled matters by himself mounting a coup in order to apply his concept of neo-liberalism in an authoritarian manner. In Algeria, in January 1992, the military authorities acted in the same way when the people, out of despair, gave massive support to an Islamic party. Must we sacrifice democracy in order to save the market?

The countries of the South are being drowned by this deluge of 'world Westernisation'. This Western success has led a historian to say that: *'All the under-developed countries of the globe have been converted to the religions of industry and wealth, and their faith surpasses that of their catechists. Never in the course of all the thousands of years of contact between the civilisations has any one of them met with such universal success.*[18] Such a fascination with the North at a time when areas of anomy are increasing in the South (in Sudan, Ethiopia, Somalia, Liberia and Mozambique...) encourages many people to emigrate towards what, despite everything, would appear to be the poles of prosperity on our planet, and, more specifically, towards the United States and Europe. Very often they attempt to enter these countries illegally. In Europe, this atmosphere of crisis (20 million unemployed within the EEC, 40 million poor people) has concentrated all possible forms of bitterness upon these illegal immigrants; from the left to the far-right parties condemn these intruders and call for them to be sent back to where they came from. Beyond the illegal immigrants it is of course the immigrant groups of long-standing who are being targeted. The neo-fascist language of the extreme right makes explicit reference to them (concealing other forms of racism behind a populist exterior) and thus achieves a new legitimacy. In France, for example, the National Front's proposals with regard to immigration are supported by more than a third of all French people, whereas barely 14% of them voted for the party itself in the regional elections in March 1992.

According to the sociologist Pierre Bourdieu, such an attitude bears a certain relationship to the economist dogmatism prevalent in society: *'The consequences of a policy conceived as the management of economic equilibria (in the narrowest sense of the term) must be paid for in many ways, in the form of social and psychological costs, in the form of unemployment, illness, delinquency, addiction to alcohol or drugs, of suffering which encourages resentment and racism and leads to political demoralisation...'.*[19]

People have the feeling that their misfortune is too great and that the authorities are too distant; they do not feel that they are recognised or listened to by those who have the power to act or to protest. The media, in particular, – and above all television – which could explain, analyse and promote civic feeling, instead contribute to worsening the chaos. Pierre Bourdieu comments: *'No day passes without us seeing the same small group of interchangeable actors debating the same interchangeable points of view on topical issues'.*[20]

Today, the 'fourth estate', for long seen as a popular resort against the three others, has been tainted by suspicion. The whole business of Romania, the Gulf and other more recent events such as the Habache affair, have convinced people that the media no longer represent any guarantee of truth and, indeed, that the right to information – something which is essential in a democracy – is endangered.[21]

Looking beyond the media, the world appears to be gripped by an 'anxiety for information' under the influence of those thousands of information networks which convey, in real time, millions of facts and statistics from all the corners of the earth and which interconnect telephone, computer and the television screen, printers and fax machines. This results in a fascinating and disturbing technological bewilderment.[22]

It is like a drug which stimulates and stunts at one and the same time. How can we protect ourselves from these modern invasions forced upon us by progress and by the worship of performance and speed?

The Faustian threshold

Faced with the collision of all these crises, people sense that there are new human rights which must be fought for, and that a generation of new rights, guaranteeing people the right to information, to peace and to security, but also the right to purity of water and air and the protection of the environment must take over from the generation of political and social rights.

This theme of the environment, once seen as a separate issue, is increasingly understood as integral to all aspects of life. Environmental protection has become an imperative common to all societies. The conviction that the planet is in danger has become the major political trump card of this end of the century. Rather than thinking of the world in terms of economic parameters as neo-liberal dogmatism does, should we not be beginning to rebuild it on the basis of ecological data? *'The idea that monetary evaluation indicates the degree of growth and development would henceforth appear to be called into doubt,'* says Alexander King, *'energy is the driving force of the economy, and it is the only absolute; money is but a substitute.'*[23]

Energy consumption, however, continues to be extremely unequal. According to a report by the World Resources Institute, in 1984, the seven most highly developed OECD countries consumed 43% of the world's production of combustible fossil fuels and a major part of the products of the forest. Such a figure quite literally makes the idea of aligning the planet as a whole on the basis of the consumption norms of the rich absurd. The latter, the rich nations, total some 500 million, the rest, 4 thousand million. All the planet's resources would be inadequate. It is for this reason that, on the eve of the opening of the Rio conference a growing number of political leaders are realising that the old East-West confrontation was nothing in comparison with the North-South confrontation which might well be precipitated unless something is done soon with regard to the environment.

For the first time the debate with regard to climatic change is at the top of the political agenda; and the people of the West must admit that progress can no longer be expressed in terms of a surplus of happiness. We would appear to have reached the Faustian threshold.[24] Once we cross this bridge, ghosts will come to haunt us. *'Today we must abandon the idea that techno-industrial growth can bring nothing but good,'* says Edgar Morin. *'Our societies believed they were advancing along an historic motorway towards a happy future. Today, we have to modify the route, we must enrich and render more complex the concept of development. In any case, we have lost the guarantee of the future, not only in those places where communism reigned but everywhere.'*[25]

A society of waste must be succeeded by a society of sharing. After the years of financial euphoria, of hustling and swindles, it is not unnatural that we should sense a strong desire for a return to virtuous activities and to true values. Ethics, work, competence, honesty, frugality... The foundation and leaven of a new humanism. In a confused way, ordinary people see that it is the only way to save the planet, to save nature, to consolidate democracy and to save mankind. Can we rebuild the world in any other way?

* This article was originally published in *Le Monde diplomatique*, May 1992, and was entitled 'Un monde à reconstruire'.

Notes

1. Cf. the dossier 'Why the Gloom?', *Time*, 13 January 1992.
2. *Time*, 20 April 1992.
3. Alexander King, 'La voie holistique vers une société globale', *Revue internationale des sciences sociales*, no. 131, Paris, February 1992.
4. *El Pais*, 14 April 1992.
5. Interview with Edgar Morin, *Globe*, March 1992.
6. Cf. Claude Julien, 'Alerte: nationalismes!', *Le Monde diplomatique*, January 1990.
7. Alexander King, *op cit.*
8. Interview with Andre Gorz, *Le Monde*, 14 April 1992.
9. Cf. Interview with Alain Ehrenberg, *Capital*, April 1992.
10. *El Pais*, 16 April 1992.
11. *Le Monde*, 11 April 1992.
12. Cf. Stefan Dab, *La Débacle des caisses d'épargne americaines*, Editions de l'Université de Bruxelles, 1992.
13. John Kenneth Galbraith, *Brève histoire de l'euphorie financière*, Le Seuil, Paris 1992.
14. *Libération*, 27 February 1992.
15. Jean-François Revel, *Le Regain démocratique*, Fayard, Paris, 1992.
16. *Le Monde*, 4 April 1992 (supplément *Léonardo*, page 118).
17. *Libération*, 8 April 1992.
18. David S. Landes, l'Europe téchnicienne, Gallimard, Paris, 1975.
19. Interview with Pierre Bourdieu, *Politis*, April 1992.
20. *Ibid.*
21. Cf. *'Médias, mensonges et démocratie'*, *Manière de voir*, no. 14, February 1992, *Le Monde diplomatique*.
22. Cf. Jacques Lesourne, 'Futuribles européens', *Futuribles*, January 1992.
23. Alexander King, *op. cit.*
24. See 'L'homme en danger de science?', *Manière de voir*, no. 15, *Le Monde diplomatique*, May 1992.
25. Interview with Edgar Morin, *op. cit.*

3. On Listening to the British

DAPHNE HAMPSON

On being asked to write something for a European publication I find myself writing unashamedly as a British person. I say 'British', not Scottish, Welsh or English, for I am myself English but I have spent the last eighteen years north of the border (living in Scotland). I think that the various things which I have to say apply moreover equally to the various peoples living in mainland Britain. (Northern Ireland may be a different case.) It is odd to me to be writing in English for publication on the Continent, for I always try when I am able to speak the language of the people I am among when I am abroad and I do not particularly want English to become the language of Continental Europe. For this alone I want to apologise, not for anything I write in this essay. Nevertheless I have been very hesitant as to whether I should contribute to a book on 'discernment' and 'commitment' in Europe; I have allowed myself to be persuaded that I should indeed do so.

I should say something of myself. During my teens and twenties I had frequent contact with Europe, much more than did many other British people of my generation. I went to school in France for some weeks when I was 14 and between that age and 26, when I first went to the United States, I think I was in Europe every year. I went to work camps and conferences and made friends. Indeed Europe was I think an escape from England. I thus spoke French fairly well by the time I was in my early twenties when I commenced on learning German. I remember where I started. I was at a workcamp in Germany, the first time I had been there. It was the early '60s and the war still less than 20 years away. I hurt my foot and had to spend days on my back with my leg in the air. I had a World Council of Churches prayer book with prayers in English, French and German. The first German I knew was the Lord's Prayer by heart!

Aged 22, having traipsed around Europe with a rucksack on my back and visited museums, art galleries and historical sites, I gained a First Class degree in Modern History. I went to Oxford to do research and spent the next four years working on the response in Britain to the Church struggle (Kirchenkampf) in the Third Reich. I spent years poring over documents from the German Foreign Office (Auswärtiges Amt), the German Churches, and at the World Council of Churches in Geneva. Part way through this research Philip Potter offered me a job as a research assistant to him in Geneva: I think he must have concluded that I knew the history of the ecumenical movement and modern church history as well as anyone else around – and that was just about true. I wanted however to remain an academic. I was one of the first to start working for the ordination of women in the Anglican churches in Britain, and consequently I was invited to WCC consultations in Geneva and in Strasbourg.

It did not seem strange to me therefore when with the foundation of the European Society of Women for Theological Research (now called in English the European Society of Women *in* Theological Research) in 1986 I was elected the first and founding president (or co-ordinator as I often called myself then). My experience with the European Society was very mixed. It was extraordinarily hard work. I virtually put my career and my research on one side as I worked for it for two years. In some ways of course it was a joy. I met some fine people. But I also found it one of the more difficult experiences of my life, and it is about that that I shall have reason to speak in this essay. The experience lies behind some of the judgements that I have come to form. I have also had other happier experiences of Europe in recent years. In particular in 1984 I was invited to the then DDR (East Germany) as a guest of the theology faculty at the Karl Marx University in Leipzig. An odd invitation – that a theology faculty of a university with such a name should invite a radical feminist theologian to give a lecture on 'Die Herausforderung des Feminismus für das Christentum' ('The Challenge of Feminism to Christianity')!

Nevertheless I have to say that despite all this experience of the continent I do not see myself as committing myself to Europe at this stage. I want to explore why that is so. Europe has become a place for holidays but not for work! (I still apparently use the word 'Europe' as excluding Britain and have difficulty in grasping that that is now no longer the case.) How am I to make the transition to seeing myself as a 'European theologian' and what prevents it? Suppose I was to be given the opportunity to go and lecture in some western European countries (East Germany was much easier) under the ERASMUS scheme. Would I go? Yes I suppose so: but not without considerable trepidation. I do feel I live in a different world, with different presuppositions and values. To name them exactly is the difficulty.

Let me start by saying that I am not a Christian. Yes I am a systematic theologian, a proper 'Systematikerin' (it sounds better in German), teaching theology at a good and ancient theology faculty in a Scottish University. I am the first woman to be employed permanently and full time in a divinity faculty which dates back to before the Reformation, that at the University of St. Andrews. That is all just fine, and I enjoy it. It is indeed unusual not to be a Christian in such a situation, but it is not impossible. Our presuppositions and our academic arrangements in Britain allow for such an eventuality. University faculties are not tied to the churches. We do not have a concordat. It is not that the churches retain control over theology faculties. I do not have to see a bishop, or be approved by some church council before I may teach. There are some odd arrangements left over from the past, whereby a professor at a university like mine is indeed appointed by both the university and representatives of the church. But it is the university that pays the salary almost in totality and therefore it is the party which calls the tune. Nor are such committees necessarily partisan: in Edinburgh the Presbyterian Church committee concurred some years back now with the filling of the chair of systematic theology by a Roman Catholic. (And I myself am not a professor, so there is no church involvement in my position.)

I think that the difference here must be one of the first things which a British person approaching Europe (and particularly the Dutch and German academic worlds) notices. Theology faculties on the Continent seem to be tied to the church in a way which is unimaginable in Britain. The church appears (to me as a British person) as a kind of deadweight, determining what is possible and what is not. Again, theology seems to be the servant of the church. It would interest me to know, in Germany or in the Netherlands, what proportion of young people training in theology at their universities will be ordained or enter religious orders? Of the undergraduates who study with me (for theology is a first degree subject here which one can study straight from school) no more than 10-15% intend to be ordained. The rest will become lawyers and bankers and teachers and social workers and anything else which you can do after leaving university with a good 'Arts' degree. Most of my students are Christians, but not by any means all. (Some these days are feminists!) More significantly I often do not know, or only gradually discover, what a person's religious allegiance is.

Theology, then, is a university subject in its own right with its own field of enquiry. Theological faculties are not an adjunct of the church. They may be useful to the church. Many of those seeking to be ordained have enjoyed studying with me. I have written references for a young man who wished to enter the Dominican order and listened to a woman trying to find a way forward in the 'male' Presbyterian church, which despite ordaining women seemed to have no place for her. Human beings seek to counsel one another and as a teacher it is my duty and my privilege to listen to all kinds and conditions of persons. But my students know perfectly well that I am not myself a Christian. The diversity which exists makes conversation real, among students and between students and myself. A young person studying theology will be exposed to people with many different spiritualities and positions. That is what makes the class room exciting. People learn tolerance and respect for others. A theology faculty is, at best, a place where people are free to grow and change; to find out who they are and to become themselves.

My sense here of 'Europe' is in this respect very different, and perhaps I generalise from too few examples. I should like to be proved wrong. I was invited, as the post-Christian feminist which I am, to come to a congress of Christian women in Liverpool. Would I lead a workshop on post-Christian feminism? I wrote back explaining my views (again) and making sure that they really wished me to come – to what was advisedly an assembly of Christian women. Yes they knew perfectly well what it was that I think and would I please give my workshop. I did. Many people came. Among the audience on that occasion was one of the speakers at the conference. Elisabeth Moltmann-Wendel. I was glad to see

Elisabeth again and enjoyed her presence as she sat quietly in the audience observing this group of British women. Afterwards she told me that she did not think that such a situation would be possible in Germany. I was fascinated. I wish now that I had taken down her words. But it was something to do with the tolerance exercised towards a different point of view.

Indeed I am perfectly at peace in the company of my British friends who are theologians and who are Christians working within the church. Since I came out against Christianity, there has been no break in personal relations between me and any single woman (or man) who has remained in the church. The only woman who has attacked me in print in an unjustifiable manner without first clearly stating what it is that I think is, I am sorry to say, a German woman living in Britain. I have had no 'Auseinandersetzung' with anyone. Nor is this chance. It has been the habit of British people that often those of the most contrasting views in theology have been friends, this among male theologians and stretching a long way back. There are debates, but it is because friendships are possible that debates can also been carried on in a meaningful way. Thus in recent years I have debated either on the radio or at public meetings with a number of the leading Christian feminist theologians in Britain. They have always been civil, indeed enjoyable occasions. A body such as the Movement for the Ordination of Women (in the Church of England) no less, invited me to their Annual General Meeting to put forward the view in debate that feminism and Christianity are not compatible.

There is moreover a very different theological tradition in Britain – and this again makes it possible for someone like me to function as I do in a British theology faculty. Philosophy of religion has always been strong here. That is to say the question is raised as to the truth of Christianity. What impresses me then about German dogmatics – say the work of Jürgen Moltmann to take an example – is that it takes place within a 'theological circle'. I want to say a theological 'small' circle. Therefore it strikes me as very conservative and as not asking the right questions. Let me explain. The answer as to whether anything can or cannot be said (whether it is true or not), it seems to be presumed, lies in whether or not it is in the bible, or present in church tradition. Thus (for example) one may find a whole exposition on the doctrine of the trinity (including a consideration as to whether God is not a 'motherly father', which would bring us up to date), without the question in any way being posed as to whether the doctrine of the trinity is true!

It almost seems as though the Continent, or parts of the Continental tradition, has by-passed (or not wanted to look at) the questions over which debates have raged in Britain during the last twenty or more years. Where is the Continental equivalent of for example, *The Myth of God Incarnate* (ed. John Hick, SCM press, 1977)? But if a debate has once taken place, as it has within Britain, as to whether we can still talk in terms of 'incarnation', or whether it is not the case that this is a dogma which simply reflects a particular set of historical circumstances, it is no longer possible simply to go on reiterating these supposed truths as though they were self-evident. The conservatives in Britain too have these days to take account of the debate and to put forward an apologetic for their belief. Again in relation to the bible. The speed with which Continental theologians, including notably feminist theologians, simply revert to telling me that something is in the bible (as though that were then the end of the matter) amazes me. Take for a recent, and Catholic, example, Catherina Halkes' *New Creation*. The early chapters of this book open up every question under the sun. But then she seems without further ado to assume that whatever is in the bible is right: the object of the exercise becomes to find a biblical verse which will substantiate whatever it is that she wishes to say.

Is there no tradition in (Continental) European theology of being able to stand outside the text, outside the tradition, to ask questions of it? That this takes place in Britain has come about, I think, through the presence of two disciplines. Firstly I mention philosophy of religion, which has kept theology on its toes through asking all the really difficult questions. And secondly, and no less importantly, the strength of historical theology within this country, such that the study of the fundamental doctrines of Christianity has taken place with reference to the historical context in which they arose. This interface with other disciplines means that systematic theology in Britain has to find its feet in dialogue with other disciplines. I would take one further example of such an interface: the long-standing debate which there has been between science and theology in Britain, stretching back to the nineteenth century. Theology is called to give an account of itself. It cannot just continue to proclaim 'the word of God' – and to exegete Genesis as though Darwin had never lived. It must explain what it is that it wishes to say in terms which make sense to the world at large. Finally the fact that theology exists within a public context in Britain has I believe been important here. I myself have frequently been on the radio for example. Bishops sit in the House of Lords. There is a wide arena of public debate about theological questions. (I notice this by contrast in particular with the United States, where almost no intelligent public debate about theology takes place.)

Furthermore there is something else at work – which I think I have already hinted at and which makes me proud to be British. There is clearly in Britain a long-standing tradition of democracy and stability and complexity to our national life which makes it possible for a person to think what he or she will. I find there thus to be (Northern Ireland here would be a different case) a very great tolerance of differing points of view. This indeed is a primary reason why I choose to live in Britain rather than for example in the States. (I have my doctorate in theology from Harvard and have spent many years in the States, so it was fully possible that I might have decided to emigrate.) I notice this not least among feminists. At least in the States, there are certain things which you are supposed to think if you are a feminist. For example it would be a heresy of proportions which would almost put you outside the feminist community to think that the difference between men and women might in some way owe to biology and not just be a product of social conditioning! Again, you have to be in favour (it is compulsory) of the opinion that homosexuality is a possible ethical option. Most American feminists tend to belong to a school – and the post-modernists have little to do with the followers of Carol Gilligan and so forth. Not so in Britain: there is a real freedom to think out what it is that one oneself thinks as an individual. I am suspicious of Europe. I am not quite sure what is the case. But I sense that there is a certain bandwagon going, perhaps in regard to holding certain views about the Third World, or even as to whether we should be interested in women in the past, which views you had better accept if you do not as a feminist want to be ostracised.

I think that in all this it has in the British situation been immensely helpful that we have had a complex religious geography. We never had a situation, such as resulted from the Thirty Years War in Germany, whereby the prince of a principality determined what its religion should be. It is not the case, as in the Netherlands, that there are basically just two traditions, Protestant and Catholic. (In my younger days wanting to stay at the Bahnhofsmission on occasion I never knew how to answer the initial question 'Protestant or Catholic?' I was at the time Anglican!) We have had many different denominations and traditions, and this since the seventeenth century at least. This has fractured and broken open the situation in a way which makes all kinds of things possible. This is often not realised by people on the Continent, who often assume for example that all English people are Anglican! No: a census taken in mid-Victorian England showed about half the population to be Anglican, the rest was divided between the many other churches. This has not changed, though there has been a relative rise in the number of Roman Catholics, and fall in number of Free Church people. In Scotland where the Presbyterian church is the 'state' religion – though no church is established in Scotland in the way in which the Church of England is in England – there is a large body of Roman Catholics. This very diversity has I think been profoundly helpful.

Where are women to find themselves in the complexity of the new Europe? How does the kind of diversity and openness of which I am speaking apply to them? Again I write as a British woman, and one who had a relatively bad experience as president of a European organisation of women, which has left me with a lot to think about. I think that I should want to say three things. Firstly that women (and more generally Europeans working in theology, but I am thinking specifically of women here) need to learn how to listen to one another. Secondly that women should make sure that, with all the differences and tensions which are potentially present, they keep to the best democratic traditions which we have. Thirdly that women (and men also) need to allow space for individuals to be themselves, and the cultural contexts out of which people come to be diverse. This, of course, reverts to the need to listen to one another. I shall try to speak to each of these in turn and to draw on my own experience, however painful that may have been.

Firstly, the need to learn how to listen. I am increasingly convinced as I get older (!) that the ability to listen is the mark of human maturity. It is as a person has a centredness in herself or himself that she or he is able to be open to and to listen to other people. The inability to be attentive to others is the mark of immaturity. (Men have often indeed shown their insecurity through their relative inability to listen to women and in thinking that they need to dominate the conversation.) I want to say here that the women whom I most treasure, of whom I have the best memories, from the years when I was in the Christian church or on the edge of it, are older women in every case: I think of a French woman, a German woman from what was then the DDR and a Swiss woman whom I hardly knew but whose image is still before my mind as I write. Why? Because I think they had seen life and experienced pain (they had all in one way or another taken extraordinarily courageous actions during the years of the Third Reich or under Communism) and this had in every case promoted a quiet centredness in self and an openness towards other people. With such women I could be comfortable: they were my friends. There flashes into my mind a conversation with an Alsatian woman, Elizabeth Behr-Sigel, Orthodox in religion no less; and the amazement of an American running a World Council of Churches programme at what good friends we were despite the difference in religion (for I was already very radical) and at the happy way in which we communicated in a mixture of three languages in a veritable tower of Babel, settling on German as the best *lingua franca* between us.

But such experiences have been the exception and by no means the rule. I have not always found younger Continental women able to be present to others in this way. I have found them to be impetuous and lacking discernment. I remember when I was arguing that Israel should not be admitted to the European Society without great thought (for it was not a European country and admitting Israel would cause major problems as to who should then be admitted), but rather be given associate status. Instead of this being able to be talked through in reasonable fashion in relation to geography and what it might mean for other non-European countries I was simply told (by one German woman) that what I was saying owed to my 'insular' British views. I agree that Britain has a very different history in relation to the Near East. We had, not least, an association with Palestine in the days before the creation of Israel as a state. Again, we have a large population of Muslims these days in Britain – with all the questions which that brings to the fore as to whether, if there was a branch of a society in Israel, then we should not have to admit Palestinian Christians also (and whether that would be possible in the circumstances of Israel); and if Palestinian Christians then why not also Palestinian Muslims? The thing was as complex as could be. But therefore all perceptions needed to be listened to carefully. It was no place for slinging off-hand and rude remarks at people.

Secondly I would point to the need for women to foster democracy. 'Democracy' here need not necessarily mean all the paraphernalia of votes and points of order and standardised agendas which we have inherited. Women have, quite rightly, been suspicious of some of the ways in which men have conducted meetings in the past. Too often there has been a simple counting of votes without any attempt at consensus decision making. The best decision is not necessarily the majority decision. It may be very important to take account of minority views and needs. Moreover the best decision is not always apparent to anyone at first. More time and thought may be needed until the whole group can come to a solution of which no one had initially thought. Quakers[1], among whom I have spent much time in recent years, have since the seventeenth century practiced a form of decision making which is other than straightforward democracy. They try to take the mind of the meeting under God. Likewise women have in recent years, for example in the peace movement and in innumerable conferences, successfully worked in a way which is new. They have listened to one another. They have tried to include all. They have sought to find a way forward which does not set up an antithesis of those in favour and those against. It can be that women conduct business in a much more informal atmosphere than do men as a rule and are more efficient as a result.

The problem to which however I am pointing here is captured by the title of an early article which emanated from the women's movement: 'The Tyranny of Structurelessness'. It is crucial that women learn to abide by the spirit of the informal structures which are present. Structurelessness can lead to chaos. It can allow the domination of a meeting by a group which is unscrupulous in its fanaticism and who exploit the situation to their own ends. I have seen this happen in the most appalling way. What interested me was that in the instance of which I am thinking it was British Quakers who came to the microphone advocating that the meeting should conduct its business with a wider vision and in a more constructive way. I have never been so clear in my life as to where my allegiance lay. There is a way of conducting affairs which involves keeping calm amid diverse claims and waiting until the way forward can be discerned. It takes a maturity of mind and of judgment to be able to do that. I admire it when I see it.

What is needed here is trust. If people choose to disrupt a group in the interest of sectarian ends we cannot have an international community. Any organisation, having set up some people in authority, needs then to support that leadership and to act responsibly. Again we revert to the need for listening. It is as women are attentive to one another that they are enabled to find a way forward. Particularly among religious people, it ought to be axiomatic that we think of the common good, our sensitivities finely attuned. It is not only men who can dominate women. Women can dominate women. They can also on occasion behave with less maturity than a gathering of men would be inclined to exercise. For men behave impersonally, they conform to rather rigid structures, and the result is that no one gets hurt (if little is achieved). Women can be so emotional and perhaps so fraught from the circumstances pertaining in their lives that they may throw reasoned judgment and honourable behaviour to the winds. Restraint is of the essence of the matter, especially in an organisation in which we are struggling with different languages and presuppositions.

And so I turn thirdly to the need to give space to individuals to be themselves. There are very different cultures operating in this regard within Europe. I remember being astonished at an international workcamp (I think it was in Germany) in the early '60s (and I remember the other British people commenting on this too) where it seemed to be supposed by some of the Continental people present that we all had to do the same thing – whether that was to go to the swimming pool or to play games! The British people took it for granted that when we had free time we should each go our own way and do what we wished to do, maybe in groups, maybe alone. Germans at that time were much aware of the fact that they must foster 'democratic decisions'. But this seemed to involve voting on everything and thinking that, at the end of the day, we should all do the same thing. Therein lay no freedom! Surely live and let live is what is called for in such circumstances: I speak as a British person. Again, I have felt criticised (at a meeting in the Netherlands) because I did not dress in the style expected by Dutch feminists. But as a British woman who is a feminist there is no particular way in which I feel obliged to dress – and if I enjoy smart clothes (and have a few) there is no earthly reason why I should not wear them. I am allowed to be old-fashioned. We need to cherish the fact that people are diverse.

The cause of the strife may well be the very self-consciousness of feminists, who are trying to create something new. Many women are insecure. They are in jobs which may cease to exist. They have not had years of academic training behind them as have their male colleagues. They are setting out to do something which is decidedly against the 'male' establishment. They may be unused to public meetings and positions of influence. But then coming to have these things is liable to go to their heads like wine! The result can be spectacularly difficult. Again in the British situation I think that we have been better off here. For it is not particularly rare for a woman to be a university lecturer (Dozentin) and a theologian. There have been women teaching in British theology faculties for many years now. The women's colleges in Oxford and Cambridge were founded at the end of last century. I gather that it is something much more recent for women to be teaching at universities for example in the Netherlands. Of course the academics in British universities are not necessarily feminists. But there are a good number of women in positions of influence and this is nothing new. We have therefore been absorbed into academic life and academic ways of doing things. We achieved our doctorates at the same kind of age as did our male colleagues. This has been immensely helpful and puts Britain in a different situation than European countries where the advent of women as theologians is radically new.

Finally I would want to say that it is of paramount importance in international situations to be polite to other people, to show them respect and courtesy. It is no good behaving in a bombastic way, supposing that everyone from another European country, which maybe has very different traditions, will necessarily interact in group situations as one would expect at home. Thus I remember sitting at an international meeting with a group of French women, baffled and in one case in tears, at the way in which they had been treated. They needed others to be patient and forbearing, giving them the respect which was their due. Another example. I was about to chair an international meeting and no one could be found even to help me with the most elementary things like finding felt-tip pens or drawing pins (thumb tacks). It is only as we are sensitive to the needs of others and are supportive of them that the whole can go forward. We need to watch, observe, listen and to help. It is imperative that we say 'thank you' when it is due.

Perhaps it will strike people as odd that these things do not always happen. But they are far from axiomatic. I have seen people go behind the backs of others and set up counter-groups, try to undermine people, yell at others, and behave in the most atrocious ways. At the worst I have been led to think that I understood how it was possible that Nazi Germany could get under way on the Continent (and why it could not have in Britain). Nor was it only people of German extraction who were behaving in this way. Elementary civil courtesy does seem to exist in Britain. I have never known that not to be the case. That has not always been my experience of the Continent. As a result people can be badly damaged by behaviour meted out to them by others. The effect may be felt long after the event. I was moved to think indeed that I had been privileged to learn something of what it must have earlier been like to have been a Jew, isolated, ganged up against and cut down. It was terrifying. And I know that I am not the only one who has been hurt.

There may be differences of tradition here, but that does not mean that it is helpful to import them into international situations. I have been told, by a British woman living in the Netherlands, that some measure of abusiveness is how Dutch women will often treat each other. They have a great row, she said, and then all go off to the pub together. Again I have been told (though I have not experienced this) that there has been the most awful antagonism in Germany between those who are Christians and those who follow Wicca or the Goddess. Indeed, when I was first elected as president of the European Society a Swiss woman said to me that she had been thankful to hear that a British person had been elected; she thought the rifts and splits in Germany were so deep that no German could work in that situation and bring people together for the present. I was astonished. Whom does such antagonism help?

So my experience of the European situation has been bad. I have tried and I believe failed. I worked as hard as I have ever worked in my life for an organisation and I was not so much as thanked for it. I set up an international newsletter which I edited and produced myself. (The cost to the organisation was minimal.) I corresponded with women all over Europe. Some of this of course was delightful. But no one ever knew how much time I put in. My successor as president, Mary Grey, said some nice words about the work I had done in relation to Eastern Europe in enabling women to come to the West for a conference. That was simply because I showed her those (thin) files. The files for western European countries were thick. I spent one Christmas holiday writing a constitution – which had to be in German and conform to Swiss law because we wished to have a Swiss bank account. (Women's organisations are just the same!) I tried to get financial arrangements worked out on a fair basis, given that women in some European countries had so much more money in their pockets than others. I was in many ways a slave to this movement: I worked and worked. One might have thought that at least a nice letter when finally I resigned was in order. Apparently the next conference – I was by then in the States – thought to send me a telegram. None ever arrived. Meanwhile I had received the rudest letter (in German from the Netherlands) that I had ever received in my life, criticising me for matters in relation to which I had done my level best.

Women have got to behave better than men, not worse. Feminist contexts, I have learnt, are capable of degenerating into women behaving as men would never dream of behaving. But amid this there are some saints, some women who stand out for their balance, their calm, their perspicacity and their humour. One memory comes to my mind. My friend (as she has now become) Alice Medcof who is Canadian (and had been invited to a meeting as a guest) faced me across the table; she a priest, I not a Christian. She said something about spirituality and I picked up on what she said. There was silence between us and listening, a sense for what the other meant and something held in common. She, at that conference, quietly celebrated the eucharist and I rejoiced. Some women found a way to be together in peace and to share their love of God. So there are such moments, such understandings, in situations which otherwise seem devoid of God. Again I think of a simple thing: a woman, again British, who, amid all the flurry, when we were to have a celebration, changed into a nice skirt for the evening. That simple act showed that she wanted to do something special, to be her whole self and to celebrate beauty. Amid all the hardness of things, all the debates and misunderstandings, we need people who can perform simple gestures and speak to higher values. I thank these people.

So what of the way forward? How do we become a community of women within Europe? How indeed do women and men who are religious persons find a way to be together in the new Europe which we are creating? I am sure for a start that the World Council of Churches does not hold the key. Why not? Because it is too conservative and fails to confront issues of truth. I must explain! The World Council of Churches conservative?? People will think that I am mad! Here I have to let come into play the particular opinions which I have myself, for they colour my views. Because the World Council has wanted to be radical socially and politically it has remained conservative theologically. Or is it just that, were it to succeed in keeping all churches and traditions together, the World Council dare not look at radical theology for fear of annoying the Orthodox or alienating those who think that women should not be priested? But the theological conservatism is marked. In the late '70s and early '80s the most radical social and political programmes (of which I approved) existed side by side with a Faith and Order Commission which was timidly considering orthodox views on Church, Ministry and Sacraments. That seemed to be its main theological concern. In the same years in Britain all hell had been let loose theologically. After John Robinson's *Honest to God* of 1963 there had followed *The Myth of God Incarnate* in 1977 and wide-ranging discussion (participated in by among others the Regius Professor of Theology in Cambridge – note Geoffrey Lampe's *God as Spirit* of 1977) over the fundamentals of the Christian faith.

Ecumenical Christians must get out of the habit of thinking that theology is simply to be tagged on to the radical social and political statements which they make. All too often it seems to be the case in ecumenical circles that you say what you want to say politically, or concerning the ordination of women (the field of which I had experience), and then you stick some biblical quotation on the front which would seem to support your point of view. But this simply shores up the belief that the bible contains all truth and is to be taken 'as gospel'. What if the bible does not say what you wish to say? What if the bible itself must be called to account? Until we face such issues we shall never be able to see what religion might be in the modern world. The World Council had when it was formed as its basic condition of membership (and this has now simply been amended so that it becomes a trinitarian formula) the belief (which a church which wishes to join must acknowledge) that Jesus Christ is 'God and Saviour' (sic). In Britain at least it has been this which has been so widely challenged. Many religious people, and many feminists in the church, clearly no longer believe that. The BBC promotes discussions between those who do and those who do not. I suppose it to be the case that many feminists who call themselves Christians within Europe no longer believe this either. But they have to go on with the farce of pretending that they do if they are to remain in the Christian church (and so have jobs).

We need to tackle theological questions head on. As fundamentally as we tackle political and social issues. If this is not done the doors are simply opened to all manner of weird and wonderful things – while nominally people remain Christian. Thus it would be my impression (and I may be wrong about this) that it has been the failure of the World Council of Churches to face the radical questions which have been asked in theology since the war, from Bultmann forwards, which now leaves it confused as it confronts the modern world. The reports which I heard of Canberra made it sound like an ecumenical ship without an anchor, a veritable

Noah's ark containing every opinion which liked to shelter under its roof. But the flood gates cannot be kept closed: questions which threaten theology as we have known it must be admitted. A good example here of the failure to confront modernity would be Latin American liberation theology, perhaps the most conservative theology going in the world today (while being one of the most radical socially and politically). One finds sophisticated theologians reading the scriptures in the most naive way, as though there had been no such thing as the Enlightenment or biblical criticism.

It is here that we Europeans ought to be able to help. For it is we who have been through the Enlightenment and who have had to look hard and long at the questions which it raises. No longer can we simply speak of Jesus Christ as 'God and Saviour' without asking what that means. Again, we cannot simply repeat trinitarian formulas without an acute awareness of the particular historical context out of which such theology came. We have known biblical criticism with a vengeance. No longer can we repeat John's gospel as though it came from the mouth of Jesus. The resources for a new future precisely lie in our European past. It is only by absorbing the lessons of the past that we can hope to be in a position to speak relevantly to the future. For truth will out. We can no longer repeat outworn theological formulas which we hold to uncritically while getting on with some political and social agenda. The politics and social concern would be better off without the Christian formula attached to it: the theology is simply superfluous.

One has to face the fact that someone like myself is no longer a Christian: I who was born and bred within Christendom, who in the past has twice almost been offered and nearly accepted a position at the World Council of Churches, who has been president of a European theological society. I may be an exception. But if I am an exception then I am only an exception within theological circles, in that I choose to remain a practicing theologian professionally. In the non-theological world, most of my friends think as I do. They are no longer Christians, although Christianity in the past meant a great deal to them. Some of them remain nominally in the Christian church. Others have left. One thing they hold in common. Those who are women (and I am speaking basically of my women friends) have felt a breath of fresh air in the last twenty years as women have begun to come into their own. The Christian church cannot contain them. They are too wild and free. I do not mean they behave wildly: many of my friends and I myself behave in the most sober fashion. But our thoughts have expanded beyond the theological horizons of the churches of which we were once happily a part. This is notable not least among my women students.

So what of the new world? It is not Christian I think. It may be spiritual: that is my hope. But we have got to create this new future, it will not just happen. The forces of Christendom are telling us that we should build a new Christian Europe. Not a bit of it; I hope not. That can only disadvantage women. What do we see? No sooner is Communism disestablished in Eastern Europe and Christianity is supposed to take its place than women find themselves in difficulty in having abortion rights taken seriously, while the question of whether women can be ordained is actually placed on the theological agenda again in countries where it had been thought that that had been settled in women's favour long ago. A pan-Christendom in Europe cannot but leave women as secondary citizens, as has always been the case within Christianity.

I do believe then that it is primarily women who within Europe must create a new spirituality and a new theology. The men are not going to do it. The World Council of

Churches is not poised to take action. Nor are national church institutions, and certainly not the meetings of archbishops and popes, the ecumenical councils and the whole apparatus of official Christendom. Yet women are at a disadvantage. As we have said, they hang on tenuously in (male) theology faculties. They have to receive the approbation of (male) bishops and church bodies. It is often hard not to be a Christian, indeed to come out against Christianity. Where are the funds? Where is the support? How can you have a career? We begin to see how disadvantaged are women as they try to bring about something new. The male religion still rules.

Yet I am sure that we must think with this kind of breadth if we are to find a way forward. Otherwise Europe will simply become a commercial, secular world. We need a spirituality for our future. And we need a specifically European spirituality. We have been through the Enlightenment and secularism and cannot turn to the naivity which is Latin American theology. Again, we are not the United States with its crusades and evangelism. It is within Europe that a modern world, a post-Christian spiritual world, might be enabled to come into being. The resources seem scarce. In Britain however women at least are beginning to arrive at a new synthesis. The signs are encouraging. The question remains as to how one could meet with other people in Europe who are thinking along the same lines and is not easy to think out.

The seeds of a different situation are however present in the European past. It is almost two hundred years now since Friedrich Schleiermacher had the audacity and the vision to write his *On Religion: Speeches to the Cultured Among its Despisers*. The grandfather of a modern European spiritual world (if he later became more conservative), he charted a way forward. His starting point was not any revelation, supposed to have taken place in a past age; a revelation which we may now think untenable. He had dropped the Christian myth, which churches, through their creeds, still recite. He precisely wanted to speak to the most advanced, the most cultured people of his age – and to find a way for them to be spiritual persons. It is, I believe, women who, if anyone, may be able to find a way forward from the legacy which Schleiermacher left. For women have so little stake in the specifically Christian heritage. But we must take courage.[2]

In the meantime some of the problems which I have mentioned may fade away as women come into their own. Bad behaviour is often the result of insecurity. It is as women are enabled to be themselves – and have time and space and financial resources and academic tenure – that they will be able to create a theology which reflects an inner security and which thus has about it an integrity and a sureness of touch. By the same token they may be enabled to behave in ways which are just and good and insightful towards others. Feminists are right that we need to have done with the past and to move on. But we need to move on in such a way that no one gets hurt unnecessarily. This will take a listening at which women have so often been adept, an ability to be present for the other and to truly respond to who she is and what it is that she is seeking to convey. Only in this way can we create a new Europe also in a spiritual sense.

I have suggested in this essay that British people, especially more radical British people, have much to contribute. That is difficult when the culture which one meets across the channel is such that one retreats again into one's shell. As we say 'once bitten, twice shy'. The British is a very different culture, but it has great strengths. Some of those strengths I have tried to name. At its best British culture has a breadth, a sensitivity, an openness to debate and a non-fanaticism which I applaud. This is said by someone who used to escape from Britain to 'Europe' in her youth, and who has spent many years in the United States. I have come to see that there is much which is admirable about my country. There is a deep-seated democracy here. Among feminist women this has translated into a markedly strong tolerance for people whose views are other than one's own. One of the most healing things for me after my European experience was to be invited, as a non-Christian, to the conference of British Christians which I mention. Unlike in the European situation, where there seemed to be no support, on this occasion I was able to give support to the organisers of that conference. I took on the role of being the person who collected and gave out notices at meals! It felt good to have such a humble, and useful, role – and to be accepted for who I was.

This is not an academic essay – though it contains far-reaching theological proposals. It is a feminist essay. Feminists have wanted to bring their whole selves to their work. Men do that too: though they do not realise that they write themselves into their work and then damage other people by suggesting that their outlook is absolute, if not God- given. We each only have our own experience on which to go. My experience has been part negative and part positive. It has been in part European, and yet also the result of seeing myself as a British person. It has been in part the vision of an insider, a member of a prestigious theology faculty, and yet also that of an outsider, one who is not even (!) a Christian. I am convinced however that it is only as we are able to put our views on the table and to bring our whole selves to our work, that we shall be able to think out an imaginative future. It is in that hope and with that aim that I have written. I trust that my essay will meet with response.

Notes

1. The Religious Society of Friends (Die Religiöse Gesellschaft der Freunde).
2. For a fuller exposition of my theological position see my *Theology and Feminism* (Oxford: Basil Blackwell, 1990) or my forthcoming *After Christianity?* (Philadelphia, PA: TPI and London: SCM Press).

4. The Place of the Church in the New Europe*

DUNCAN B. FORRESTER

1. What is the 'place' of the Church and of Church theology to be in the new Europe?

The concept of the 'place' of the Church was helpfully and systematically developed by Bonhoeffer, in his 1932 lecture on the nature of the Church, which echoed themes from his *Sanctorum Communio*. The Church, he argues, has lost its sense of 'place', and hence its integrity:

'It wants to be everywhere and is consequently nowhere ... Never and nowhere it is wholly itself. It exists only in disguises. It has become the world without the world's becoming the Church ... Having lost its specific place, the Church is now only to be found at privileged places in the world. It now feels more comfortable in this place rather than that ... It has lost the yard-stick for its proper place.'[1]

There is, of course, a sense in which the Church has a *given place* in space and time and society and culture. Within that given place the Church is presented with particular limits, temptations and opportunities. The given place does not determine the Church's choices, its way of being the Church, although it presents a range of specific possibilities, ways of realising the concrete and proper place of the Church within the given place in which it finds itself. It may allow itself to be drawn into captivity to its context, in which case the Church becomes part of its context, reflecting and reinforcing the dominant values and attitudes to be found there, and incapable of establishing a critical and constructive distance from its context. Or the Church may struggle to transcend its particular context and stress its own universality by striving to find its own specific place. It may choose *with whom* it is to be placed – specifically whether it is with the powerful or the powerless, with the rich or with the poor – and in this choice it is seeking to be with the Lord, the only proper place for the Church in accordance with the patristic adage, *ubi Christus ibi ecclesia*. To quote Bonhoeffer again:

'What is the Church's proper place? It is impossible to specify it concretely in advance. It is the place of the present, a contemporary Christ in the world. It is the will of God which chooses his or that place for this purpose ... No one knows in advance where this place, this centre, will be. Historically speaking it may be right on the fringe as was Galilee in the Roman Empire or Wittenberg in the sixteenth century. But God will make this place visible and everyone then has to include it in his itinerary. All that the Church can do is to attest the centre of the world which God alone decides. It must try to make space for God's work.'[2]

Because the place of the Church is not always the same, because God constantly calls his Church to new and unexpected places, it is impossible to specify the place of the Church in all ages and all cultures. But crises, times of challenge and turmoil, have the capacity to undercut conventional understandings of the place of the Church, and clarify, at least for some people, the proper place of the Church in a specific modern context. Accordingly I look backwards historically to consider two every different understandings of the place of the Church in Europe, each reinvigorated by the upheaval of a world war, each still a live option, in the hope that these may clarify what is involved in enquiring as to the place of the Church in the Europe of tomorrow, in the light of the upheavals and possibilities of today.

2. First, I want to examine the notion that the place of the Church is at the centre of things, and that Christianity ought in some sense to be 'in control' of society and culture. This may be labelled a Christendom approach, and it has a long and notable history which does not concern us here. For many it remains a desirable goal, suggesting ways in which order may be restored after periods of turmoil, fuelled, that is, not only by medieval atavism but by a vivid conviction of the public relevance and truth of Christian faith. Hilaire Belloc, although by no means a seminal thinker or a significant theologian, captured the essence of the Christendom view very lucidly in his polemical little book, *Europe and the Faith*, published in 1920 in the immediate aftermath of the First World War, when many Christian thinkers were trying to limit the damage done by that war to the faith of multitudes and to the image of Europe. Belloc's book has aged in a number of ways, and in parts it is very superficial and swashbuckling. But it is still a clear expression of an approach to the place of the Church in Europe which must be taken seriously.

For Belloc, in the divine ordering of history the unity and structure of Europe derive from the Roman Empire which merged not just with the Christian Faith but with the Catholic Church:

'For the Christian religion (then as now) was a thing, not a theory ... It was expressed in what I have called an organism, and that organism was the Catholic Church.'[3]

Thus the Catholic Church becomes the soul, the vital principle, the continuity of Europe.[4] The Catholic identity of

Europe has been challenged in the past, it is true – by the orthodox schism from the East, by Protestantism from the North, by Islam from the South and today by Marxism and secularism. But the Catholic Faith and the Catholic Church remain 'the soul of our Western civilization', and without the Faith and its essential institutional embodiment Europe would disintegrate and cease to be. Europeans (and particularly the French) are a chosen people: their Faith, their culture, their political institutions are of universal significance. Europe is the christopher, the Christ-bearer. It has been shaped by the Faith, and should continue to be so informed: hence 'Europe must return to the Faith or Europe will perish'.[5]

The past of Europe, the present identity of Europe and the European future are all tied up with the centrality of the Catholic Faith.
'Europe is the Faith and the Faith is Europe' – Belloc's slogan not only defines and limits Europe, it also suggests that the Faith is now inseparable from European culture. Its universal role is also the universal role of European civilization.

We have here, of course, a rather extreme case of culture-Christianity, where there is more than a symbiotic relationship between the Faith and European culture. Europe has become part of the essence of Christianity and Christianity cannot be engaged with without also engaging with European culture. This kind of syncretism is positively delighted in by Belloc. There is no tension between the Faith and its European home – except that the Faith (and here Belloc betrays his nostalgia for a romanticised medieval Christendom) constrains modern capitalism, materialism and acquisitiveness.

There is also in Belloc an extraordinary ecclesiastical triumphalism. The Church is without spot or wrinkle. The

Crusades, and even the Inquisition, are to be boasted of: 'Catholicism is never more alive than when it is in arms.'[6] Hildebrand 'imposed nothing on Europe. He made nothing new. What he did was to stiffen the ideal with reality. He provoked a resurrection of the flesh. He made corporate the centralised Church and the West.'[7] The Church has nothing to repent of; it is the pure soul of Europe. The mandate of the Church is Hildebrandine – to be at the heart of things, controlling, guiding, shaping Europe and directing it towards its ultimate destiny. There is no place here for pluralism, nor for a relatively powerless Church. This is *ecclesiastical* triumphalism, for the stress throughout is on the centrality and significance of the Church as a hierarchical institution beyond human questioning, and not at all on the possibility that the Church may stand under the judgement of God, that the Church may be sinful, aggressive and exploitative, that the Church may be part of the problem of Europe rather than the solution.

Belloc's dual confusion of Europe and the Christian Faith, and of the Christian Faith and the institutional Church poses problems.
These are particularly pressing when we recognize that Europe is a power complex with its own interests, which operates much as do all other powers, i.e. it pursues its own interests with rather few constraints, it has limited tolerance for radical dissent, and it rarely shows altruism or a passion for justice. To identify Europe with the Faith is no better than identifying Britain or France, or Germany, or the capitalist system, or socialism, with the Faith. It opens the way to radical perversions of Christian theology. On both counts the proper service of theology to Europe is frustrated.

3. The second approach is the polar opposite of the Christendom view as articulated by Belloc and other, abler think-

ers. It sees the proper place of the Church as being more commonly on the margins, from where it can speak truth to power and serve the life of the city more authentically than if established at the centres of power. This general understanding of the place of the Church also has a notable history, but here I content myself with indicating the position through a brief discussion of Karl Barth's attitude to Eastern Europe and the advice he gave to churches, particularly in Hungary and Czechoslovakia, in the late 1940s and early 1950s in the aftermath of the Second World War and the early days of the Cold War, as Communist regimes were being imposed on all the countries of Eastern Europe. Barth's position was controversial at the time and he was vigorously attacked not only by 'Cold Warriors' but by Reinhold Niebuhr and Emil Brunner for refusing to repeat his 'Nein' to Nazism in the face of Soviet imperialism and totalitarianism. And there is renewed controversy today, with the advantage of hindsight, as to whether Barth's advice was wise. My interest in this paper is not to provide a detailed reassessment of Barth's dealings with Eastern Europe, but rather to examine his priorities and approach in addressing the issues of Europe and the Cold War, and to ask if there are lessons for us to learn from this.

Barth's repute as an immensely influential and formative theologian and as a courageous antagonist of Hitlerism was soundly established in the 1930s. He had been the *guru* of the Confessing Church and also of the emergent ecumenical movement. For many in the immediate post-war period he was *the* theologian. His theological standing and position made it inevitable that he should address the issues of the Cold War and of the division of Europe. But what he said was unexpected and unpalatable to many. In articles, letters, and personal contacts with a wide range of friends and theological symphatisers in Eastern Europe, and in visits to Hungary (with its large Calvinist Church) Barth developed a coherent and influential position, radically opposed to that presented by Belloc after the First World War. Barth's utterances at that time need to be assessed particularly in the light of what has happened since. But that is a task for another time. Here I attempt simply to outline Barth's 'discerning of the signs of the times', in contrast to Belloc's, and to ask whether it has anything to suggest to us which is relevant to the responsibilities of today.

Barth saw the division of Europe into two hostile camps and the war to which the Cold War was the successor as clear signs of the collapse of Western civilization:
'In recent years the whole conception of a Christian civilization in the West has been pitilessly exposed as an illusion'.[8]

If the culture-Christianity of the 19th century had been a colossal distortion of the Faith, it was now more vital than ever that Christian theology must not tie itself to this problematic culture and social order. The Faith for Barth is emphatically *not* Europe. But all that is best in European culture and society is rooted in the Christian Faith, and the Church has responsibilities for Europe – as for other continents and contexts.

But what is the 'Church' that can help or even save Europe? Barth's ecclesiology is, not surprisingly, worlds apart from Belloc's:
'The real Church is the lowliest, the poorest, meanest, weakest thing that can possibly exist under God's heaven, gathered as it is around a manger and a Cross ... And the real Church is also the highest, richest, most radiant and mighty thing under God's heaven'.[9]

It lives in obedience to the living and often unexpected Word of God, and always holds itself ready for new orders. Times of turmoil represent special opportunities to hear the Word of God:

'For the Christian Church a new political system necessarily means an occasion to revise the foundations of its own activities, a challenge to renewed concentration, a summons to fresh witness, all of which is appropriate since a time of political upheaval provides the incentive to seek a better knowledge of the Word of God'.[10]

Inasfar as it looks after its own proper concerns it must be fundamentally interested in what goes on in the world, and willing if so called to enter the fray. But it must participate without abandoning its own proper freedom. It is concerned with specific political situations rather than ideologies and 'isms', and here it *witnesses* in fear and trembling. For it can no longer 'rely on the fact that it is surrounded and sustained, as it was previously, by the glory and the pathos of the culture and the politics of a Europe rapidly rising to prominence and power'.[11] It will have to learn modesty and realise that its new situation brings with it new opportunities of authenticity:

'The Church will have to learn afresh to walk towards its Lord as Peter did, not along smooth paths and up fine staircases with handsome balustrades, but on the water. It will have to learn to live on the edge of a precipice, as it did of necessity in its beginning. It must learn again how to fulfil its duty nonetheless – simply in the impetus and magnetism of its own beginning and its own aim'.[12]

That, in Barth's view, was the place of the Church in the 1950s; I suspect he would wish to affirm that its place is still 'on the edge of a precipice'. On this basis, Barth supported churches in Eastern Europe in seeking not exactly an accommodation with their governments, but as being willing to regard their lands, schools and property and so forth as dispensable. What was important was retaining – or recovering – the freedom to *be* the Church and proclaim the Gospel. The Church must not rely on the cultural or the political order to sustain it, or teach it its task. The contrast, not only with Belloc, but with the line followed by some of the churches in Eastern Europe is marked. Perhaps Barth was a little unrealistic about the need for the Church to have a material basis for its institutional existence and its freedom. And he seems almost oblivious to the advantage to churches under pressure of having outside institutional, political and ecumenical support. Certainly the Reformed Churches of Eastern Europe appear to have retained during the Communist years less freedom from political control than the Roman Catholic churches. But Barth's rejection of ecclesiastical triumphalism and his call for modesty and simplicity on the part of the churches are, I believe, of continuing significance.

Furthermore, Barth encouraged his disciples – most notably Hromadka in Czechoslovakia – in refusing to reject the new regimes, in affirming their search for social justice, and in engaging in dialogue with Marxists, a dialogue which bore fruit, including the brief experiment in 'socialism with a human face' under Dubcek in 1968, and the conversion to Christianity of a handful of leading Marxists such as Milan Machovec, the author of *A Marxist looks at Jesus*.[13] Today one may wonder whether that dialogue was direct and radical enough on the Christian side.

4. We stand in the early 1990s at an extraordinary turning point in Europe's story. Opportunities and dangers which were almost unthinkable as recently as two years ago lurk at every turn and in every country. As modern walls are torn down and people long for a broader and deeper sense of community, ancient ethnic and religious rivalries which were

for long held below the surface by despotism have emerged and reasserted themselves, opening prospects of squalid and destructive conflict and division, as well as reminding us of the extraordinary persistence of primordial loyalties. The ideological scene has been transformed in a couple of years. In the confusion and uncertainty, ultimate questions about Europe and its place in the world, and what holds Europe together, and what European identity may be, and the basis of European culture, are raised with a new urgency. And for Christians at least the place of the Christian faith and of the Christian Church must appear on the agenda.

On the assumption that theology emerges from some specifiable context, and at least at some level addresses that context, it may be helpful to detail the concrete and immediate issues which crystallized the concerns of this paper. It was initially drafted, during and after the Gulf War, as the gruesome but predictable aftermath of that conflict slowly unfolded and we became aware little by little of the extent of devastation and death this episode had produced. Many people were discussing what sort of Christian worship, if any, might be legitimate to mark the end of the Allies' direct part in the shooting and bombing and destruction. This war was celebrated by Francis Fukyama as the inauguration of a New World Order in which much of the globe will continue to be subject to bloody struggles and fruitless revolutions, while the industrial democracies – particularly the United States and the European Community – busy themselves with wealth creation in a growingly unequal world: 'with the exception of the Gulf, few regimes will have an impact – for good or ill – on the growing part of the world that is democratic and capitalist. And it is in this part of the world that we will ultimately have to make our home'.[14] Such a context raises in pressing form questions as to the place and the responsibilities of the Church and of theology in a Europe which is already one of the major power centres in the world. Similarly, the increasing and markedly visible poverty in Britain, and the growing gap between the wealthy economies such as the European Community and the poor nations of the world raise questions as to the place and responsibilities of the Church and of theology in a Europe which is a major concentration of wealth.[15] Today's context and tomorrow's possibilities make questions of the place of the Church and of church theology in the new Europe unavoidable.

5. The Christendom view is alive and well, particularly perhaps among conservative Catholic groups in Eastern Europe and the Vatican.[16] But it is not just nostalgic or triumphalistic Roman Catholics who hanker after a restored Christendom. They have their Protestant equivalents in those who hang desperately onto Establishment and, in more secular mode, those who, like Arend Th. van Leeuwen, see Western and essentially European technological culture as having a unique dynamism which is both rooted in Christianity and makes its world-wide spread a contemporary vehicle of the Christian message, or those who see a primary task of the Church as the maintenance of cohesive social values of Christian provenance now transposed into a secular idiom.[17]

A particularly impressive, consistent and influential version of the Christendom view of the future of Europe is presented by Pope John Paul II. Since before he became Pope, Karol Wojtyla, had confidently predicted the inevitable collapse of European communism, leaving a vacuum which only Christianity could fill. This prophecy became the basis for his project of a unified and re-Christianised Europe stretching from the Atlantic to the Urals, which would be in a real sense the heart of the Christian world.

This vision was most fully articulated in the Pope's 'Declaration to Europe' which he delivered in Compostella on the 9th November 1982. The place he chose was significant: Compostella was the most important pilgrimage centre in Europe, the pilgrim ways linking together the various nations of Europe and the pilgrimage itself giving some sense of European identity even when Europe was politically fragmented:

'It can be said that the European identity is not understandable without Christianity, and it is precisely in Christianity that are found those common roots by which the continent has seen its civilization mature: its culture, its dynamism, its activity, its capacity for constructive expansion in other continents as well: in a word, all that makes up its glory. And truly still, the soul of Europe remains united because, beyond its common origin, it has similar Christian and human values, such as those of the dignity of the human person, a deep sense of justice and of liberty, of industry and a spirit of initiative, of love for the family, of respect for life, of tolerance with the desire for co-operation and peace, which are notes which characterize it.'[18]

Thus the Pope held, and holds, that Europe is the continent which above all others has contributed to the development of the world. But Europe is challenged and disturbed by secularized, atheistic and materialist ideologies. Accordingly the Pope issues a passionate call to Europe:

'Find yourself again. Be yourself. Discover your origins, revive your roots. Return to those authentic values which made your history a glorious one and your present so beneficial ... you can still be the guiding light of civilization and the stimulus of progress for the world.'[19]

These notes have been sounded all over Europe by the Pope since 1982, and were at the heart of the agenda of the 1991 Synod of European Bishops. The Pope's project has been remarkably consistent; the dream of a united re-Christianized

Europe is now to be translated into reality. 'A united Europe is no longer only a dream', he said in Prague in April 1990, 'it is an actual process which cannot be purely political or economic. It has a profound cultural, spiritual and moral dimension. Christianity is at the very root of European culture.'[20]

It is not hard to find resonances here with the tradition of thought we discussed as exemplified in Belloc. The Pope is suggesting both a Christian service to Europe in its time of turmoil, confusion and uncertainty, and a restoration of the hegemony of the Church. The proper place of the Church is at the heart of things. It has only temporarily been displaced and forced to the margins by the interludes of Marxism, secularism and materialism. But the Pope tells only half the story of Europe: Europe, in his view, has brought enlightenment, culture, virtue and faith to the rest of the world. There is no mention of the slave trade, of genocide, of ruthless exploitation, of cultural and religious arrogance on the part of Christian Europe. Nor is attention given to the extent to which Christianity has been, and continues to be, a continuing major factor in European disunity. A similar one-sidedness is shown in the understanding of the Church implied in these utterances. The Church quite simply is the Roman Catholic Church, in its most ultramontane form. This Church, the Pope suggests, can guide, animate, heal and unite Europe. It has nothing to repent of, no lessons to be learned. It speaks to Europe from strength rather than weakness. It claims its proper place at the centre of things, at the heart of Europe which is itself the heart of Christendom. The message is a call for the restoration of the order of Christendom with the Christian Faith embodied in the heart and the Church at the core. It is in no sense a challenge or a disturbance to Europe, or to the Church. The place of the Church in this project is where it once was, the restoration of the proper ordering of life by the Faith, with the Church at the centre – certainly not on the edge of a precipice, or on the margins.

There is no doubt as to John Paul II's profound concern for the unity of Europe, and his conviction that Europe's destiny is to be at the heart of a restored Christendom, and to that extent he shares Belloc's vision. But he has also been at pains to stress universal or global rather than simply European issues, for example, in his 1987 Encyclical, *Sollicitudo Rei Socialis*. It is not possible for him to affirm with Belloc that the Faith is Europe; it is clearly something far greater than Europe. In the same Encyclical he vigorously attacks the blocs which divide Europe, and delivers carefully balanced critiques of both Marxist Communism and liberal Capitalism as two rather similar forms of materialist consumerism, which both involve massive distortions of authentic values and true human solidarity. His recent (1991) Encyclical *Centesimus Annus*, produced to mark the centenary of *Rerum Novarum*, has a substantial celebration of the collapse of what he calls 'real socialism', and far less criticism of Capitalism, or indeed of consumerism than before. This is perhaps partly because the focus is once again mainly on Europe and 'the year 1989' rather than the third world which was the major concern of *Sollicitudo Rei Socialis*. The overall message is unambiguous: the Church having consistently stood for justice, liberty, solidarity and human dignity, is now ready to resume its role as the sole head of Europe, guiding and directing Europe in its pre-eminent place in the world.

6. Two influential contemporary thinkers who see the place of the Church as at the margin, but also understand this as a place of opportunity, and accordingly have resonances with Barth's view, are Alasdair MacIntyre and Vaclav Havel.

Perhaps in their thought we may find some stimulus for reflection on a possible alternative role of the Church in the new Europe to that suggested by the Pope.

In the well-known conclusion to *After Virtue* MacIntyre compared our present condition to a new Dark Ages. In the old Dark Ages people of conscience and of faith learned no longer to place their hopes in the continuation of the Roman Empire, or to devote themselves to shoring it up. Instead they dedicated themselves to developing in the monasteries and in the congregations new models of community in which civilization and the moral life could be sustained and perhaps enhanced, and truth rediscovered. Since in MacIntyre's analysis we have reached a similar historical turning point, a new Dark Ages with the barbarians in power, once again the task becomes 'the construction of local forms of community within which civility and the intellectual and moral life may be sustained through the new Dark Ages that are already upon us.' And in these communities we are 'waiting not for Godot, but for another – doubtless very different – St. Benedict'.[21]

The response that MacIntyre counsels appears at first glance to be one of retreat and passivity, nostalgia and irresponsibility. But is it? The Church and people of conscience, the custodians of tradition, do not voluntarily decide to withdraw from influence over and interest in power; they have been progressively excluded as the tradition has been increasingly disregarded; and now they are simply facing their real situation, with its opportunities and dangers. This new context need not lead to passivity, despair or nostalgia. The wilderness, far from the seat of power, is a place where fresh insights may be generated, ideas for which the time will come. In the Bible the desert or wilderness is often seen as the place of disclosure and enlightenment as well as testing; even the place outside the camp where redemption is achieved for the city (e.g. Heb. 13, 12-14). New wisdom continuous with the old may well emerge in a powerless wilderness community. Fresh insights may come from the periphery.

Such communities may also be seen as experiments in faith, in virtue and in civility – all things of challenging relevance to the life of the broader society. They are communities of seekers of a city, seekers of the Kingdom of God and his justice, experimenting in structuring their life on the basis of that justice, and in the process of living it out hoping to deepen their understanding. There is also here an element of *testing*, testing God's justice to show that it works, exploring what it means to be the people of God. More is involved here than the preservation of the tradition. There is reappropriation and anticipation as well, but everything hinges on there being lively and honest communities of those who seek a city.

Such communities are not bolt-holes for the timid, but by their very existence, by the way they structure their common life, by the nature of their celebrations, a constructive protest against the established order, 'the rule of the barbarians'. They are demonstrations of the viability of another way, which insistently by their very existence question the adequacy of the community in which they are set. They point to a better way, and are themselves signs, instruments, and proleptic and partial manifestations of the Kingdom.

Furthermore, they are fellowships of expectation, aware of their own incompleteness and provisionality. Unlike utopian communes they know that they are incapable by themselves of building Jerusalem or establishing the justice of God. They *wait*. But this is not a totally open expectancy: they await a person, a new and doubtless very different St. Benedict. The person is named and this gives a clue to his role and significance. The father of monasticism and a crucial figure in Joachim's apocalyptic thought represents an older Christian tradition which is still capable of combating the new barbarism and illuminating what is going on today. And Benedict is one of the patrons of Europe, who through his development of monasticism shaped and unified Europe. The significance of this is that a serious attempt to live the Christian life, to *be* the Church made a vast, but indirect, contribution to the development of Europe. There was, in Benedict, no attempt to claim the heart of things. Monasticism spoke truth from the margins. And so it may be today ...

One waits not alone, but in fellowship with the *una sancta* that is shaped by and nurtures the ever fresh tradition, that is the Body of Christ in time and space. And the waiting that is enjoined, while it may exclude participation in the 'barbarian' polity on its own terms, is active rather than passive. It involves exploration and experiment, hard thought and risky action, in community and virtue, and costly protest against evil, injustice and oppression. This kind of waiting may be the truest service that theology and the Church can offer to the emerging European community.

Vaclav Havel saw the terminal agonies of the Maxist regimes of Eastern Europe as a symptom of a far more profound and pervasive global upheaval with its epicentre in Europe. Both East and West, he argues, are simply variant forms of consumerist industrial society. The old Communist regimes of Eastern Europe he saw as 'a kind of warning to the West, revealing its own latent tendencies'.[22] The East holds up the mirror to the West. Both are consumerist societies in a deep crisis: 'A person who has been seduced by the consumer value system, whose identity is dissolved in an amalgam of its accoutrements of mass civilization, and who has no roots in the order of being, no sense of anything higher than his or her own personal survival is a demoralized person, the system depends on his own demoralization, deepens it, is in fact a projection of it into society'.[23]

The system – and Havel clearly means both the old Eastern Marxist systems, where decadence, decay and dehumanisation are easier to discern, and the societies of the West – depends on *ideology*, the fuction of which 'is to provide people ... with the illusion that the system is in harmony with the human order and the order of the universe'.[24] Ideology legitimates power, for it pervasively suggests that 'the centre of power is identical with the centre of truth'.[25] Ideology, overtly in old Marxist societies, covertly in the West, is thus the main pillar of the system which effectively creates and *internalizes* a false reality. It 'is built upon a very unstable foundation. It is built upon lies. It works only as long as people are willing to live within the lie'.[26] While the primary reference is to the Marxist societies of the East, Havel makes it clear he is also pointing to the pervasive crisis of consumerist societies in general. Thus, *we are living within the lie.*

But it is possible, even in a totalitarian dictatorship, for individuals or groups to live in the truth, rejecting the lie, exploding the ideological justification of power by shouting that the emperor has no clothes on. The person who steps out of living within the lie 'rejects the ritual and breaks the rules of the game. He discovers once again his suppressed identity and dignity. He gives his freedom a concrete significance'.[27] This *dissent* truth is inherently a challenge to the system of lies. It involves a deep commitment to the priority of people over systems, any system. The task is dissent, resistance:
'It seems to me that all of us, East and West, face one fundamental task from which all else should follow. That task is one of resisting vigilantly, thoughtfully and attentively, but at the same time with total dedication, at every step and everywhere,

the irrational momentum of anonymous, impersonal an inhuman power – the power of ideologies, systems, apparat, bureaucracy, artifical languages and political slogans. We must resist their complex and wholly alienating pressure, whether it takes the form of consumption, advertising, repression, technology or cliché – all of which are blood brothers of fanaticism and the wellspring of totalitarian thought.'[28]

The idea of living in the truth, dwelling, abiding in the truth, as developed by Havel or Michael Polanyi, is attractive as an account of theology and of the Christian life and of the life of the Church. And living in the truth is not, and cannot be, simply an individual affair. It involves solidarity. And the community that lives in the truth cannot be introverted, partial, *incurvatus in se*. There must be an element of universality and openness to it. So the community, according to Havel, 'must foreshadow a general salvation and, thus, it is not just the expression of an introverted, selfcontained responsibility that individuals have to and for themselves alone, but responsibility to and for the *world*.'[29] This community is accordingly a parallel society, an alternative way of life. But it is not a ghetto, for the very notion of living within the truth is inescapably concerned with the welfare of others. The community is thus responsible for the world and for others. 'Responsibility is ours ... we must accept and grasp it *here, now* in this place in time and space where the Lord (sic) has set us down'.[30] Thus the parallel *polis* points beyond itself and only makes sense as an act of deepening one's responsibility to and for the whole, as a way of discovering the most appropriate *locus* for this responsibility, not as an escape from it'.[31] It is a standing challenge to the existing power structures, but it does not become a political movement seeking to wrest power for itself. It affects power only indirectly.

And this community that lives in the truth, that dissents, that resists, that explores, that represents an alternative *polis* and a different way of life is also open to the future. But unlike the ideological systems in which it is set, it does not sacrifice the present, or people, to the realization of the future. Indeed it believes that the future is already here in a partial sense, and can be grasped and lived in the present inasfar as one lives in the truth. 'The real question', writes Havel 'is whether the "brighter future" is already always so distant. What if, on the contrary, it has been here for a long time already, and only our own blindness and weakness has prevented us from seeing it around us and within us, and kept us from developing it?'[32]

This sort of account of communities of dissent is suggestive about the nature of the Church and its place in Europe. It may also be the seedbed for a style of theology, a way of life which requires a certain kind of theology. This is not an ideology which authorises systems of power by linking them to the divine order, although it is constantly being sucked towards ideology. It has less to do with internalizing obedience and reverence for the system than with sparking off questioning, dissent and resistance. Unlike ideology and grand systems of thought which appear to explain everything with their overarching interpretations, this kind of theology is usually unscientific, unsystematic – fragments, hints, clues, cries, questions, pointers, protests, comments that are generated by the the endeavour to live in the truth, acknowledging that the truth cannot be manipulated, controlled, comprehended, captured but only loved, and lived in, and revered, and worshipped.

7. In the light of the above discussion of the possible 'places' of the church in the new Europe, I want to examine and assess three recent documents – the *Declaration* 'That we may

be witnesses of Christ who has made us free' produced by the Special Assembly for Europe of the Synod of Bishops of the Roman Catholic Church and published on 14th December 1991[33]; the *Report* of the Fifth Ecumenical Encounter held jointly by the Conference of European Churches (CEC) and the Council of European Bishops' Conferences (CCEE), held in Compostela, 13-17 November 1991[34]; and the draft document *Christian Responsibility for Europe*, prepared for the European Evangelical Assembly in Budapest, March 24-30 1992[35].

a. The Synod *Declaration* takes as its starting point 'the Communist system's sudden and extraordinary collapse, in which the heroic witness of the Christian Churches played a great part'. This is portrayed as a spiritual as well as an economic and political turning point, for 'the whole of Marxism is based on an anthropological error' in reducing the human being to merely material and economic dimensions. Many of Marxism's damaging effects remain, but its collapse has highlighted the fundamental deficiencies of atheism. Atheism, the *Declaration* suggests, has shown itself to be inherently dehumanizing. But nevertheless multitudes of people in Europe 'still think and behave as if there were no God'. Thus Europe is being challenged to make a new choice for God.

European culture has deep Christian roots, the *Declaration* claims, but no longer may one say (like Belloc) that Europe and Christianity are one and the same thing. Christianity may have given Europe its fundamental principles and its sense of identity, but in recent centuries there have been strenuous efforts to detach European values and principles, and indeed its public life generally, from Christian roots, basing them instead on secular rationality. These modern alternative foundations have now, the *Declaration* suggests, been shown to be frail and unreliable. Hence there arises a need for a style of evangelization which is not the restoration of the past, but a challenge to Europe 'to uncover its Christian roots and to build a more profound civilization, clearly more Christian and therefore more richly human' (II.3.). Europe is to be renewed through a fresh dialogue with the Gospel, which must be 'inculturated' in Europe, if it is to provide an effective and strong response to modernity and 'so-called post-modernity'. This in its turn will strenghthen true humanitarianism, encourage 'communion' (not 'solidarity' – the Pope's favourite term!), and help to challenge the values of consumerism.

In this task of re-evangelization, all Christians must work together, and the opportunities and problems of relationships with the Orthodox and Protestant churches, with the Jewish people, and with 'all those who believe in God' are laid out in fairly bland but uncompromising fashion.

A major concern of the document is the restoration of 'the Church's strength' (V). Parishes are vital in this regard, as is catechesis. Catholic schools and universities and other institutions require to be restored. The re-evangelization of Europe, it appears, involves necessarily the recovery of the former institutional standing of the Church, of 'the Church's strength'. A condition of this restoration is complete loyalty to the official teaching of the Church: in rather ominous words the *Declaration* claims that 'theological "dissent" is an obstacle to carrying out evangelization, particularly evangelization within the Church' (11). The forces that will re-evangelize Europe, it appears, must be strictly disciplined, obeying orders from above without question. It is this kind of statement, together with the establishment of a Roman hierarchy for Russia, which alarms the Orthodox, and led to major Orthodox churches declining to send fraternal delegates to the Synod.

The Church's teaching, it is affirmed, has much to contribute to Europe; it, and it alone, is capable of filling the vacuum left by the collapse of Marxism. While the Church does not present any 'Christian model of society', it 'favours a correctly understood democracy' (IV), and 'approves the usefulness of a market economy and free trade', provided that their introduction into the nations of Eastern Europe is carried out 'with sound reasoning' – which appears to include measures to protect the dignity of workers and to encourage their participation in the businesses in which they work. Basic principles particularly commended to the new Europe are human dignity and human rights, subsidiarity and the solidarity which has become a major slogan of the present Pope. The social teaching of the Church is therefore to be taught and commended.

Finally, there is a somewhat cursory acknowledgement that the history of Europe 'has known many dark moments', among which imperalism and the economic exploitation of other countries are mentioned. Poor people from the southern parts of the world 'are constantly clamouring for a bold and effective solidarity against hunger, many difficulties and the injustices which afflict them'. (V) Europe, the *Declaration* suggests, should respond with prudence to the cry from the South, and to the problem of economic migration into Europe – which merits a paragraph to itself.

Commentary must start with noting that some key passages of the *Declaration* are more than a little simplistic. The analysis of the collapse of the East European Marxist regimes, to give a central example, is far briefer than that in *Centesimus Annus*, and even more naive in its account of the causes of this extraordinary event. If the *Declaration* represents the bishops' attempt to discern the signs of the times and adapt their leadership style accordingly, it is positively alarming in its superficiality. Similarly, the account of Europe's economic relations with the rest of the world fails to take full account of structures of injustice and exploitation and is likely to encourage a complacency which could be extremely dangerous. It encourages the idea that the systemic injustices of international economic relations may be solved by solidarity, compassion and charity; there is no mention either of repentance or of the need for radical change in the international economic order. But perhaps most serious of all is the fact that there is so little in the *Declaration* which is *theological* wrestling with the situation with its vast potential for good or ill. An account of the opportunities open to the institutional Church in itself hardly counts as theological reflection!

While the *Declaration* on the whole affirms, as one would expect, papal pronouncements on Europe, and particularly *Centesimus Annus*, it also appears calculated to qualify the more triumphalistic comments of the Pope on Europe. But this laudable and necessary task is undertaken in such a half-hearted way that it does not suggest any serious need for repentance on the part of Europe, or of the Church. The document even mentioned the five hundredth anniversary of 'the evangelization of the Americas' as if this were an unambiguous achievement of Christian Europe! Such simplicities do not serve the world Church well, and understandably dismay many Christians in the Americas.

Finally, while the *Declaration* in effect commends the catholic social teaching which has become the political theory of Christian Democracy in Europe, as usual it declines to suggest that these same principles might have some bearing on the structure and working of the Roman Catholic Church. In a time of uncertainty, when old systems and ideologies have collapsed, there is certainly a challenge to the Church to suggest what might be the basic principles of the new Europe. There is also much to be said in favour of the principles commended by the *Declaration*. But it would be much more impressive if the Roman Catholic Church endeavoured to show in its own life that these principles are valid, and work. But just the contrary is in fact happening. The subsidiarity, democracy, and participation in the exercise of power commended to secular systems seem the opposite of the increasingly authoritarian monarchical centralization in the Roman Catholic Church. Similarly the support for freedom and the acceptance of pluralism commended to secular societies are seemingly contradicted both by the drastic treatment meted out to theological dissenters (particularly those who raise the issue of the authority structure of the Church), and by the increasingly half-hearted ecumenism emanating from Rome. Despite some fine words, the main message of the *Declaration* seems to be that the re-evangelization of Europe and the restoration of Christian Europe are Roman Catholic responsibilities and, one must add, opportunities. Indeed, if Peter Hebblethwaite's account is to be relied upon, the Pope has determined to replace the CCEE, the Organization of European Bishops' Conferences, with an entirely new organization under more direct Vatican oversight as the body responsible for the evangelization of Europe.[36] It would be strange if many people, and particularly the non-Roman Catholic churches of Europe, were not rather worried by such developments.

b. The fifth Ecumenical Encounter was organized by the Council of European Bishops' Conferences and the Conference of European Churches and accordingly included Orthodox, Protestant and Anglican representatives as well as Roman Catholics. The Encounter was thus thoroughly ecumenical, and this was reflected in the less triumphalistic tone adopted, and in the Encounter's recognition that the

Christian churches of Europe in their rivalries and divisions have contributed significantly to the bitter and dangerous divisons of Europe. Indeed, the Christian contribution to Europe was presented as so mixed and ambiguous that penitence was the necessary prelude to any constructive contribution to the future of Europe.

The evangelization of Europe was the theme that brought the representatives of the churches to Compostela, but the Encounter saw effective evangelism as depending on a new relationship being established among the churches of Europe. The danger that the old 'confessional battlelines' might be re-established was squarely faced, as was the fact that minority churches often felt a sense of being oppressed by majority confessions. Accordingly the Encounter affirmed that 'without ecumenical peace there will be neither joint evangelization nor joint witness in Europe' (par. 9). The churches were called to renounce rivalry and 'all competitive forms of evangelism' (par. 15), and to encourage ecumenical measures such as 'the ecumenical training of pastors and laity'. (par. 10)

The Compostela meeting was chastened in tone, when compared with the *Declaration* of the Bishops' Synod. It acknowledged a share of ecclesiastical responsibility for the key problems of Europe today, and seemed to accept and embrace a pluralistic Europe: it is the proclamation of the grace of God for all men and women'. (par. 11) But despite these welcome qualities, the Compostela Encounter produced rather little interesting and creative reading of 'the signs of the times', and few if any fresh theological insights.

c. The draft on 'Christian Responsibility in Europe' prepared for the European Evangelical Assembly has a distinctive tone. It starts with a clear acknowledgement of ecclesiastical guilt for colluding in, condoning, or even creating many of the problems that Europe faces today. Nevertheless, the churches wish 'to reaffirm our evangelical responsibilities for the state, society and the economy', and also to recognize the complexity of the situation consequent upon the downfall of the communist regimes: *'The transformations in Europe have made us aware of the guilt that has accumulated in our midst in the last few decades. In the East European countries a discussion has begun [on] who should be held responsible for the harm inflicted upon us by the communist system and how to treat those who supported injustice in the name of that system. The churches, too, have to face up to the question of how far they were involved. In both East and West, we must deal with the facts of injustice vis-à-vis the poor nations of the South, and of the destructive exploitation of nature'. (par. 8)*

The West is not seen as 'the lucky proprietor of the necessary solutions for the problems of the East'; radically new thinking is called for in both East and West. The danger is that the vacuum which has been left by the breakdown of the communist system may be 'a fertile ground for fanatic[al] nationalisms', and, even more threatening, 'the ideology of unlimited industrial growth and consumption in both East and West' (par. 9), based on an arrogant individualism.

In this new context, the fundamental Christian task is the proclamation of the gospel. This gospel has, down the centuries, made a deep impression on Europe, but we may no longer talk of a Christian Europe, and the Christian tradition has lost much of its impact. In an increasingly secularized and pluralistic Europe, the churches must resist the temptations of yearning for a restoration of Christendom. Rather, they should enter into a discerning encounter with the secularized world, recognizing that secularization is an ambiguous phenomenon and is capable of liberating people from prejudices, taboos, and superstition as well as of destroying things that are of ultimate value (pars. 17-18). The gospel is not concerned with the re-establishment of a Christian Europe, the formation of Christian states, or the restoration of confessions and their rivalries (pars. 21-22). Instead, the gospel must be proclaimed and offered in a humble, non-authoritarian way as a contribution to the future of a Europe whose pluralism is accepted and affirmed (par. 27).

'Christian Responsibility' is far more circumspect in what it says about the market economy than is the Synod *Declaration*. 'Free competition,' it says, 'usually disfavours the weak', and requires regulation to protect the vulnerable (par. 38): 'The churches will have to persist [in] supporting measures that soften the unavoidable hardships of the market economic system' (par. 39). Even more seriously, 'the system seems to completely fail when it comes to the poverty of the countries of the South' (par. 39), and it creates recalcitrant economic problems in relation to which 'experience shows that in many instances ideologically hardened concepts of freedom prevent the necessary measures from being taken' (par. 40).

In such a context, the task for the churches is to affirm their responsibility for what goes on in the public realm, to acknowledge their share of guilt for what has gone wrong in the near and distant past, to examine afresh what the gospel – and particularly the Reformation message of justification – means for today, to seek 'a more profound understanding of the mission of the Church' and, in close fellowship and cooperation with each other, to witness to the gospel and serve the new Europe.

This statement combines a tone of ecclesiastical modesty with serious *theological* engagement. The churches must accept with penitence that they have a responsibility for much of the evil that has happened to Europe, and this reinforces the conviction that their message must point not to themselves but to the grace and forgiveness of God. The statement has a discriminating and cautious analysis of the collapse of the communist regimes, and sees clear dangers on the road ahead. It explicitly rejects restorationism, and is willing to accept secular pluralism as within the purposes of God without capitulating to it, or allowing it to set the theological agenda. The churches have an awesome responsibility for the future of Europe. But their task is to be servants, not masters. There is an openness here to the insight of Fr. Fergus Kerr: 'Christians, in Europe at least, are perhaps more of an obstacle in the way than any kind of focus of integration ... it is tempting to suggest that if there were a lot less religion around it would be easier to see how Europeans might be united in peace and prosperity'.[37] Christians, and the churches, must be renewed if they are adequately to serve Europe. And renewal comes through the 'repentant memory' of which Kerr speaks.[38] The statement agrees with Vass that 'the future European Church will live permanently in the *diaspora of a pluralistic society*'.[39] But a diaspora Church has special opportunities and continuing responsibilities for the society and culture in which it finds its place. A diaspora Church in a pluralistic Europe, striving to be faithful to the gospel and responsible in the public realm – that seems to be the underlying vision of the statement.

8. The Church will perform the most authentic service to the New Europe if, setting resolutely aside all ecclesiastical and European triumphalism, it makes manifest its membership in the *una sancta* and uses faithfully and courageously its minority status and marginality in Europe.

It is not triumphalistic to suggest that the Church is called to be a sign of and demonstration of true community, in Europe as elsewhere. Within the Body, hostilities and oppositions are overcome and forgiveness and reconciliation are to be a present reality. But the common experience of the Church is very different. In Northern Ireland, for example, the two sharply polarised communities understand themselves in religious terms, and see the conflict as at least in part a matter of theological and ecclesiastical confrontation and opposed understandings. Thus, as Enda McDonagh points out, the one baptism which at the formal level the churches share and acknowledge, as a social reality is understood as affiliating people to opposed and often warring political traditions. 'Baptism in the Catholic Church normally signals membership of the nationalist community, baptism in any of the Protestant Churches, membership of the Unionist community. Membership and unity in the body of Christ, which is baptism's primary meaning, is exposed to frustration by its social and political significance in Northern Ireland'.[40] Not dissimilar situations, where Christian communities reinforce rather than questioning ethnic, class or linguistic suspicions and hostilities and deny in practice the unity of the Church, frustrating a fully effective Christian contribution to the unity of Europe are to be found elsewhere. McDonagh advocates an important symbolic response to the 'frustration and futility' of baptism in Northern Ireland, which has such ominous political implications: either stop baptizing, or insist that in every baptism all the Christian churches in the locality are actively and visibly involved. The integrity of the Church demands that radical steps should be taken wherever the Church in fact reinforces division and hostility.

Within the Body, as John Donne points out, we are implicated with one another, responsible for one another, accountable to one another:
'The Church is Catholike, universal, so are all her Actions'; wrote John Donne, 'All that she does, belongs to all. When she

baptizes a child, that action concerns me; for that child is thereby connected to that Head which is my Head too, and engraffed into that body whereof I am a member. And when she buries a Man, that action concerns me'.[41]

This means that the churches in Europe are accountable to God and the *oikumene* for the way they exercise their responsibilities in and to the European Community. And beyond the worldwide institutional Church there is the broader 'Church' of those with whom Christ identifies in a special way, the poor, the weak and the marginalized: *ubi Christus ibi ecclesia*. The European churches are also accountable for their life and witness to this 'Church'. And this makes it impossible for them to be at ease in a place which is clearly one of the great centres of power and wealth in the world today.

*Part of this chapter has appeared as an article in *Modern Churchman* and is reproduced by permission of the editor.

Notes

1. D. Bonhoeffer, *Das Wesen der Kirche* (Kaiser Traktate 3, ed. O. Dudzus, Munich, 1971), p. 31, cited in U. Duchrow, *Global Economy: A Confessional Issue for the Churches*. Geneva, WCC, 1987, pp. 21-2.
2. Ibid.
3. H. Belloc, *Europe and the Faith*. London, Burns & Oates, 1962, p. 42.
4. Ibid. p. 168.
5. Ibid. p. 186.
6. Ibid. p. 173.
7. Ibid. p. 149.
8. Karl Barth, *Against the Stream*. London, SCM Press, 1954, p. 57.
9. Ibid. p. 65.
10. Ibid. p. 84.
11. Ibid. p. 175.
12. Ibid. p. 175.
13. Milan Machovec, *A Marxist Looks at Jesus*. ET London, Darton, Longman & Tod, 1976.
14. *Guardian*. 7th September 1990.
15. On this see Duchrow, *Global Economy: A Confessional Issue for the Churches*.

16. See Roger Scruton, 'The New Right in Central Europe I – Czechoslovakia', and 'II – Poland and Hungary', *Political Studies* (1988) XXXVI 449-462 and 638-658.
17. Arend Th. van Leeuwen, *Christianity in World History*. London, Edinburgh House Press, 1964, and D.B. Forrester, *Beliefs, Values and Policies*, Clarendon, 1989.
18. *L'Observatore Romano* Weekly English edition, 29th November 1982, page 6.
19. Ibid.
20. *Guardian*. 27th April 1990.
21. Alasdair MacIntyre, *After Virtue*. London, Duckworth, 1981, p. 245.
22. Vaclav Havel, *Living in Truth*, London 1987, page 54.
23. Ibid. p. 62.
24. Ibid. p. 43.
25. Ibid. p. 39.
26. Ibid. p. 50.
27. Ibid. p. 55.
28. Ibid. p. 153.
29. Ibid. p. 103.
30. Ibid. p. 104.
31. Ibid. p. 104.
32. Ibid. p. 118.
33. 'Synod Declaration', in the Bishops' Conferences of Great Britain, *Briefing* Vol. 22 No. 1 (16th January 1982).
34. ' "At Thy World": Mission and Evangelization in Europe Today.' Report on the Fifth Ecumenical Encounter in *Catholic International* Vol. 3. No. 2, 15-31 January 1992, pp. 87-93.
35. *Christian Responsibility for Europe* in preparation for the European Evangelical Assembly in Budapest, March 24th-30th, 1992 (typescript).
36. Peter Hebblethwaite, 'The Pope's European Arm', *The Tablet*, 15th Februaty 1992.
37. Fergus Kerr, 'Christian Memory and National Consciousness', *New Blackfriars*, January 1992, p. 14.
38. Ibid. p. 19.
39. George Vass, SJ, 'The Christian Scene in Eastern Europe', *New Blackfriars*, January 1992, p. 66.
40. Arend Th. van Leeuwen, *Christianity in World History*, London, Edinburgh House Press, 1964, and D.B. Forrester, *Beliefs, Values and Policies*, Clarendon, 1989.
41. John Donne, *Mediation XVII*.

5. Nation-hood and Theology: Europe's Heritage Revisited

PETER SEDGWICK

1. 1914 – an alliance of theology and nationalism

The late twentieth century saw an abandonment by political theorists of the concept that the natural unit of geo-politics, or the international political order, was the nation-state.[1] From the unification of Italy and Germany in the 1860's, through the disintegration of the Austro-Hungarian and Turkish empires in the early twentieth century, the assumption was that the nation-state was the natural, or normal, unit of society. It was taken for granted that the Austro-Hungarian and Turkish empires were unstable, because they were made up of a number of ethnic groups, each of which desired to express their self-determination by forming a nation-state. Any empire which was dissolvable into a series of nation-states, and where each nationality was held together against its will, was seen by political theorists to be moving against the tide of history.

The Marxist concept of historical materialism was explicitly determinist, since it argued that the logic of economic development would result in a crisis of capitalist monopolies, where economic competition would result in a cataclysmic debacle of financial instability and growing unemployment. At this point the proletariat could seize power, if only the vanguard of the revolution had read the economic indications correctly. That was the role of the Communist (or Bolshevik) party.[2] The concept of nationalism was implicitly determinist. It was believed that the artistic and educational achievements of a people formed a unity which would guide the political and economic developments of that region. There was much talk in 1900 of the 'manifest destiny' of the American nation, which was a justification of imperialism.[3] Similar sentiments could be found in most Western European nations. It was especially the case in music, literature and art (in particular sculpture) that this outpouring of nationalism was found.[4]

In so far as Harnack, Ritschl and other theologians believed that religion was a matter of value judgements, which was the predominant tendency in the late nineteenth century Protestantism in Europe, they looked with favour on artistic self-determination. In philosophical terms, the value judgement was not only the categorical imperative (morality) but aesthetic. The neo-Kantian followers of Lötze thus found a unity between religion and culture, in which religion expressed the transcendent aspirations of that longing for harmony and wholeness characteristic of the final flowering of late nineteenth century romantic music, art and literature.[5] Nationalism was accepted as the particular self-expression of that search for spiritual meaning, but the task of religion was (in Harnack's classic phrase from *The Essence of Christianity*) to preach 'the fatherhood of God and the brotherhood of man'. There was not necessarily a contradiction between nationalism and religion. Nationalism expressed the spiritual yearnings of a particular people. It was often the case, as in Czechoslovakia, that in fact there were several people, Czechs, Slovaks and Germans, living under Austro-Hungarian rule but they were Protestant, and the history of the Protestant Reformation (the Battle of the White Mountain, the defenestration of Prague, etc) was also the history of self-determination and the vain struggle for national liberty. The belief of Protestant theologians was that nationalism was a benign force, which would allow different cultures to live together valuing their differences, but not essentially in competition with one another. Overarching this vision was a Protestant theology of divine providence, which saw in the history of religion the gradual emergence of a purified understanding of the nature of morality and God's will upon earth.[6] It was a theology of Kingdom-building, before Schweitzer's rude challenge to this view of the Kingdom.

Even before Schweitzer's attack on the idea of the Kingdom as something built by human beings, even before Barth's celebrated repudiation of Harnack's support for Germany in August, 1914, there were two difficulties with this cultural synthesis of religion and nationalism. One concerned Roman Catholicism, Pan-Slavism and the place of Russia; the other concerned revolutionary violence. There had always been an antipathy between Protestant understandings of nationalism and Roman Catholic. Catholicism was concerned with an organic hierarchical ordering of the internal nature of society. In many ways *Rerum Novarum*, Leo XIII's encyclical of 1891, was profoundly conservative, and feared the 'agitators' would exploit (in its words) the unhappy lot of the working-classes.[7] Since Austria was a Catholic empire, and since Italy had by its forced unification made the Pope 'a prisoner in the Vatican', Catholic social ethics was suspicious of nationalism. However pan-Slavism in Russia was actively hostile to the West, believing that the modernisation of Russia was a disaster for the Russian spirit (or soul). Pan-Slavism used Orthodoxy as a vehicle against modernisation, and forged a Russian nationalism which was profoundly hostile to the liberal Protestantism of early twentieth century Germany, Czechoslovakia, England or Scotland.[8] Thus, apart from the Marxist refusal to accept the price of rapid industrialisation in Russia, there was a very different disenchantment which stemmed from a quite other union of Orthodoxy and slavic nationalism. This violently opposed Protestantism and liberal culture.

The other problem with nationalism was of course its potential violence. Lloyd George in England from 1906-1918 epitomises the ambiguity of liberal nationalism. He introduced many social reforms before 1914, but once war broke out he became unreservedly a war-lord, sweeping aside those who hesitated to use its force. Clemenceau is another French example. Much socialism was deeply anticlerical, and antireligious. Like Protestantism, it believed nationalism could be beneficial, but it feared both the harnessing of nationalism by military and capitalist forces, and the perceived falsehood of religion. It opposed the alliance of Church and State found in such Catholic empires as Austria, and believed that liberal Protestant theologians had not taken their critique of false religion far enough. As Jean Jaurès, the leader of the French socialist party put the matter in 1899, 'Even if the idea of God were to assume a tangible form, if God himself were to arise visibly over the masses, the first duty of man would be to deny obedience and to treat Him as an equal with whom one discusses.'[9]

It was not however religion which killed Jaurès, but nationalism. Jaurès called for a general strike on behalf of the Socialist International once war had broken out in 1914. He was assassinated by a nationalist who believed that he was placing his country in danger. What was surprising was just how far their commitment to the nation-state had been carried by liberal Protestant theologians. After 1914, the reaction against romanticism in music, literature and art went alongside Barth's denunciation of liberal Protestantism.

This led to a profound irony in the history of Europe. The period 1918-1920 saw the rebirth of many nation-states in Eastern and South-Eastern Europe. Yet the intellectual justification of their raison d'être had changed. Their culture was treasured as their particular heritage, but it was no longer seen as forming a spiritual unity with religion. Nor was it regarded as determining the particular political or economic developments which each nation-state would seek. Culture became divided into that which was from the past (folkmusic, nineteenth century composers, past literature, art, architecture) and that which was part of the modernist culture of the twentieth century: abstract, atonal, conflictual, even surrealist.[10] There seemed no place for religion, except on its own terms, which neo-orthodoxy was happy to accept, and no place for the nation-state, except as a safeguard for the political liberties of its people. Even that was doubtful in some Eastern European states in the 1930s. So the nation-state became the natural unit of political discourse because there was no alternative. No one wanted to return to the pre-1914 empires, and no one wanted the new fascist dictatorships. It became the case that the nation-state was seen as the 'natural unit' of the political order, but the philosophical and religious justification for it which existed before 1914 was increasingly regarded as an anachronism in the twentieth century. However, since there was no philosophical or theological alternative to it, it remained the base-line of political discourse until the late twentieth century. Indeed, the history of African decolonialism is the history of the conjoining of various tribes with very different cultures into 'nation-states' by their European masters, which were then launched into political independence. The result has been repeatedly a series of national civil wars, which are in fact tribal wars. Africa saw the disastrous export of the idea of nationhood.

I do not intend to chart the well-known growth of European integration after 1945. What is far more significant for this paper is the debate between theologians after 1945 on the continuing legitimacy of the nation-state, and it is to the debate between H. Thielicke, W. Pannenberg, Roman Catholic theologians and others that we now turn. At long last the idea of the nation-state was not held to be sacrosanct.

2. *National Sovereignty: A Theological Perspective*

Gordon Dunstan, an English Anglican ethicist, argued in 1967 that the Biblical revelation places the sovereignty of God over the sovereignty of the State. This is not the placing of one sovereignty above another, but rather is the inevitable outcome of theological argument. The foundation of Biblical revelation is the sovereignty of God, which therefore that revelation witnesses to. Such a witness points to the divine judgement on national self-assertion. It is not therefore a matter of ranking divine sovereignty above national sovereignty, but rather that national sovereignty can and does manifest itself in national aggrandizement. It becomes a matter of human pride and self-will.[11]

The Old Testament vision in Amos, Chapters 1 and 2, is of a universalism where the countries of Damascus, Gaza, Tyre, Edom, Ammon and Moab are comdemned for their cruelty. These countries are clearly not nation-states in the modern sense, but they are nevertheless put under judgement. That judgement was given further moral development by Paul's exposition in Romans of a universal understanding of morality, even by nations which did not know God. It was yet further developed by the Greek understanding of transcendence, whereby the possibility of a Christian philosophy of history and society was applied to the different realms of politics, economies and culture. Such a tradition was, in Dunstan's view, distorted by being translated into particular forms of sovereignty, which eventually became the medieval concept of Christendom. The collapse of that embodiment of transcendence led to the rise of the modern, sovereign nation-state. Nevertheless, the past tradition can still be of use. The concept of transcendence can be applied as a critique of absolute national sovereignty. In particular, the idea of unitary sovereignty, where there is one head which must be obeyed, is to be resisted. So Dunstan argues for a concept of justice which would relativise the claims of particular jurisdictions. Equally sovereignty is symbolic of divine sovereignty, which is an authority placed over all nations. There is an irreducible universalism here. So 'the notion of absolute national sovereignty must be designated an aberration', in Dunstan's words.[12] This is not a matter of political expediency, nor the acceptance of an inevitable interconnectedness in economic terms, but the recovery of the theological tradition itself.

A similar rehabilitation of the pre-Reformation tradition, without seeking to recreate medieval Christendom, is found in Roman Catholic writing in the 1950s-1960s, especially in Jacques Maritain, and the papal and conciliar documents of the 1960s (*Pacem in Terris* – 1963; *Gaudium et Spes* – 1965; *Populorum Progressio* – 1967). It is a deeply symbolic vision, where these symbolic concepts provide the guidelines for an understanding of political order. The symbol of the perfect society is taken over from Aristotle into neo-Thomism, which has been the primary discourse of the Catholic church this century. The perfect society is a comprehensive concept which contains the other concepts of subsidiarity and the common good. The perfect society is the context in which humanity can fully develop its innate potentiality, including of course the worship of God. It is self-sufficient and without defects. Maritain argued in *Man and the State* that self-governed societies eventually ceased to be peaceful or self-sufficient: these two factors were interconnected.[13] They therefore needed to be supplanted by more global understandings of sovereignty which could approximate to the ideas of peace and self-sufficiency. Both of these concepts were clearly an integral part of social perfection. Equally international organisations, which embody a perfect society in embryo, may need to exercise jurisdiction and the moral obligations which nation-states had previously performed, as it were, 'on behalf of' the perfect society. The basic political reality suddenly ceases to be the State. This is only the administrative instrument of the 'body politic'. This is made up of the people, in their manifold local expressions of culture, politics and economics. Authority belongs to this manifold reality. It is delegated, but never ceded, to the State. Therefore international, or supranational unity emerges out of the social nature of human beings. All cultural organisations are potentially universal, at least in their capacity for being related one to another, and all have political significance. Since authority is located in the body politic, the idea both of the common good and of subsidiarity follow naturally.[14]

Maritain's political theology clearly influenced the Catholic Church's documents of the 1960s. *Pacem in Terris* noted the inability of the present system of political authority to correspond 'to the objective requirements of the universal common good' (para 135). *Gaudium et Spes* offered a definition of the common good which led inexorably to the abandonment of the nation-state as the sole, or even primary, unit of political discourse. 'Every day human interdependence tightens and spreads by degrees over the whole world. As a result the common good, that is, the sum of those conditions of social life which allow social groups and their individual members relatively thorough and ready access to their own fulfilment, today takes on an increasingly universal complexion and consequently involves rights and duties with respect to the whole human race' (para 26). However, that does not mean positively the development of the world government. Instead the universality of the common good means negatively a criticism of nationalism (which Catholicism had never welcomed anyway). Also the principle of subsidiarity means that all public functions should be exercised at the lowest level possible. Only when that is not possible, because local or regional government is unable to execute those functions, should higher levels be substituted. In the past that would have meant (and still often does mean) the nation-state. But issues of war and peace, justice (especially the regulation of multinationals), and the issue of rights or duties point to much bigger organisations. So *Populorum Progressio* (para 78) points to the question of how juridical and political disputes can be managed effectively. That implies a world public authority. As Theodore Weber says 'The potential of the human race, grounded in natural law, is unification on a global scale. It is thus communality of natural law, transcending all historic differences, that alllows the proponents of this view to refer to humankind as 'a family', despite the fact that empirically it quite obviously is not a family, and to forecast and work for its coming oneness.'

It is significant however that W. Pannenberg emphasises that any notion of Christian culture (as part of the movement beyond the nation-state) must be post-Enlightenment. Pannenberg has drawn attention in several books to the wars of religion in the sixteenth century. As medieval Christendom disintegrated, political theorists and rulers drew the conclusion that society had to be built on a basis that abstracted from religious disputes. So, although by the nineteenth century liberal Protestantism could legitimate nationalism as part of culture, the nation-state become from the Reformation onwards implicitly secular. The Enlightenment was, in Pannenberg's words, 'not so much an assault upon religion as an attempt to tame and universalise it for civic purposes.' Pannenberg resists any attempt 'to re-establish a pre-Enlightenment connection between Christianity and European culture.' He fears that some Roman Catholic theologians, including at times Pope John Paul II, would wish to do this.[15] Equally he is critical of Barth's influence upon German Protestantism, which means that it remains very divorced from any engagement in political culture. One such representative here would be H. Thielicke. In the 1950s and 1960s, Thielicke justified the nation-state as 'an institutional expression of the divided world.' Since the world is for Thielicke fallen and scattered by God's judgement, the state becomes the way in which chaos is held at bay. The world is viewed as being the arena of power, violence and egoism. Any attempt to move to a supra-national, let alone world state, would be in Thielicke's words 'a pseudo-messianic imitation of this kingdom, a demonic revolt.' While there may be provisional and temporary international agreements between states, and even international institutions, sovereignty remains with the nation-state. Thielicke's pessimism reflects not only the context of the Cold War, when he wrote in the 1950s and 1960s. It also reflects his deep estrangement from politics and culture as expressive of any divine revelation at all. While human nature may reach an imperfect solidarity in its family life, recreation and art, the will to power quickly corrupts any political order. It is only by God's mercy that the nation-state holds back the chaos. In Thielicke's view, the covenant with Noah is symbolic of all political life: there shall be no more total destruction, for God has given the human race the means to restrain its own capacity for evil. That means is the nation-state. It is a very limited view of politics, and even more so of the move beyond the nation-state.[16]

What we see in these theological debates is an attempt to move beyond the nation-state as the natural unit of political life. Thielicke represents the outworking of German Protestantism's reaction to the liberal embracing of culture and nationalism by theologians before 1914. In effect he is saying that the nation-state must exist, but it is no more than a regrettable necessity. It is owed little allegiance (although one may be called to die for it), and it can become demonic. Yet it must exist, because the world is as fallen as it is. Dunstan uses the concepts of sovereignty and transcendence to offer a critique of national self-sufficiency. It is not merely that in the modern world the nation-state is increasingly related to other nation-states. Much more, the Christian tradition is universalist and incompatible with too self-sufficient a particularity. Local participation in small-scale communities is for Dunstan what the Christian tradition witnesses to. However, these must never seek to become closed, or to evolve into national self-aggrandizement.

Maritain and the Catholic documents of the 1960s offer a vision from a completely different world, where the emphasis is entirely on the universal and the global. It is also very much an exposition where culture and politics intertwine, each manifesting the divine call to the perfect society. It certainly marks the end of the nation-state, but what will replace it? It is this point that concerns W. Pannenberg. Is this in fact now being taken up as a pre-Enlightenment reinstatement of Christian Europe? Are the churches capable of working with the emerging European states, while respecting their autonomy and their modernity? The answer is by no means clear. Yet the political forces making for European integration become ever more powerful. It is to this development that we finally turn.

3. *Europe 1992*

The changes in Europe in the last decade took the British people unawares. For most people in Britain the discussion in the 1970s and early 1980s was still within the bounds of national sovereignty. As the economist Andrew Britton puts it, 'The history of British relations with the European Economic Community is one of indecision and procrastination. We joined the community itself very late; we did not become full members of the European Monetary System when it was set up; now we are unwilling to sign the Social Charter or to accept the plan for a single currency.' Britton shows how the UK government argued in 1989-1990 that the European Social Charter usurped the authority belonging properly to the nation-states which made up the European Community. There was an acceptance by British industry and finance of the benefits of economic integration, and some disillusionment with a purely national economic policy. As in France, the internal political debate over economic policy was resolved by making European integration the principal object of government. The Single European Act of 1986 thus became in Britain and France the way in which internal economic difficulties were settled, and particular debates transcended: it said nothing about the future political developments of Europe.

Equally it could be argued that the Social Charter (itself only a declaratory document, in the continental legal tradition, establishing rights and obligations in general terms) did not commit the European Community to any new political development, except insofar as the rights it declared went beyond the policy of an individual nation-state. The notion of industrial collaboration, central to the Social Charter, comes out of the positive experience of Germany. However, what the Charter did do was to maintain the relationship between economics and social philosophy, which Karl Polanyi had argued for after 1945.[17] The role of the Churches here was in assessing principles and rights. The concepts of participation and the common good led Christian ethicists to argue for the opportunity of workers to join in decisions which affected their lives. Once again this approach stems from the medieval Catholic tradition, in which broad principles advocating the common good are the basis for action.

Therefore the Single European Act and the Social Charter (which was embodied in the Social Chapter at Maastricht on December 11, 1991) did not represent any real challenges to the idea of the nation-state, except insofar as the Social Chapter overrode the internal sovereignty of a national government. The one is an economic development, the other is a widening of the collaborative traditions of European Christian and Social Democracy. The Social Chapter stands firmly in the tradition of the 'perfect society', where the nation-state yields some of its powers to a wider community. What did represent a much greater change was the adoption at Maastricht in December 1991 of a series of proposals:

a. European citizenship;
b. an inter-governmental common foreign and security policy 'which might in time lead to a common defence';
c. a commitment to an economic and monetary union by 1999, among those countries that reach the qualification threshold;
d. modestly enhanced powers for the European parliament.

In particular, the objective of the Maastricht treaty replaced those of the Treaty of Rome, which set up the EEC in 1956. Rome spoke of promoting 'an increase in stability, an accelerated standard of living and closer relations between the States belonging to it'. Two of the Maastricht objectives (articles B and 2) are 'to strengthen the protection of the rights and interests of the nationals of its Member States, through the introduction of a citizenship of the Union' and 'to develop a close cooperation on home affairs and in the judicial field.' What would govern this development would be the rights and freedoms 'as guaranteed by the European Convention for the Protection of Human Rights and Fundamental Freedoms, as they result from the constitutional traditions common to the Member States as general principles of Community Law.' (articles F, 3, 36).

The existence of the nation-state therefore becomes a specific limitation on the emerging European Union, or what is called in the Treaty 'an ever closer union among the people of Europe.' There would in fact have been the phrase 'Union with a federal goal', proposed by the Dutch presidency of the European Community, but it was removed on British insistence. The 'ever closer union' must have 'due regard to the national identity of its Member States, whose systems of government are founded on the principles of democracy.' Subsidiarity is defined by the Community for the first time (article 36), whereby the Community 'shall take action in accordance with the principle of subsidiarity.' 'The Community shall take action ... only if and insofar as the objectives by the Member States can therefore, by reason of the scale or effects of the proposed action, be better achieved by the Community.' Indeed, judicial and home affairs remain matters for the nation-states, but they pledged themselves to cooperation in many areas, such as civil and criminal matters.

Maastricht did not herald the end of the European nation-state. In the words of one Dutch official at the summit, it 'will win no beauty prizes' for symmetry on collaboration between nation-states; the community development of social policies which will require compliance by its nation-states; the promotion of Community citizenship; and the development of longterm Community policies irrespective of the wishes of some of its nation-states. In short, the philosophy of the independent nation-state lay behind the 1956 Treaty of Rome. What was needed was that European nation-states should no longer fight, but cooperate. The 1991 Maastricht Treaty speaks of 'an ever closer union', subject to the limitations of subsidiarity, which means that the nation-state must still be allowed to function where it can do so. Rome expressed a clear cut philosophy of nationhood with cooperation; Maastricht, perhaps inevitably, is far more ambiguous.

There is nonetheless an historic turning point at Maastricht, which is why I have given a detailed exegesis of the text. At many points the text still speaks of inter-governmental cooperation in the spirit of Rome, and the matter is further complicated by the right of nation-states to secede from the Social Chapter on some issues, as Britain intends to do. How far this right can be exercised will be a matter for the European Court of Justice. Nevertheless the concept of European Citizenship, of 'ever closer union' and the possibility of common defence through the Western European Union means that the nation-state is no longer the sole concept for political discourse.

Theologians have written very little on this matter, preferring for understandable reasons to look at some of the issues which surround Maastricht. These are first the relationship of the Community to the Third World in terms of trade (the Lomé Convention), migration and overseas aid. Secondly there is the moral responsibility of the Community to nurture the fragile democracy of the newly liberated countries of Eastern Europe, which must largely depend on their relationship to the Community. Thirdly there is the issue of poverty within the Community, and the extent to which some countries within the Community will be regarded as sources of cheap labour. Finally there is the question of the future of Christianity itself within the Community: the crisis of values, as it is often put.

Yet the issue of nation building, and the end of the nation-state as the sole unit of geo-political discourse, runs through all of these questions.

The issue of justice becomes the central issue in much of the criticism of the new Europe. Any shift from the nation-state to what in effect becomes a federal Europe is also a shift to a fortress Europe, if it erects barriers to the outside world. It also becomes a divided society, where rich and poor no longer share a common home. These concerns were especially expressed in the European Ecumenical Assembly which met in Basel in May 1989. It included representatives of Protestant, Catholic and Orthodox churches from every country in Europe except Albania.

The responsibility of affluence to the poor of the world will shape the values and character of the new supra-national order which will succeed the nation-state. The poor are not homogeneous, but they share the characteristic of vulnerability. Around the growing affluence of the European Community, and the increasing economic efficiency of its capitalist system (symbolised by the Bundesbank in Germany) there stands the fragile democracies of the East, the subsistence economies of the South, and within and without the Community the lowpaid, the refugees and the disadvantaged.

The character of the new supra-national Europe is not yet defined. It draws on the stability and peace of the last 46 years inside the Community, but in the two years since the end of Communist rule in the East many small wars have broken out. The character of the new state thus has to draw a balance between regionalism and subsidiarity, while transcending the autonomy of the nation-state. It is however in its commitment to world development and Eastern Europe that the issue of social justice will most be faced, while the Community provides a bastion of stability in a fragmented world.

Without attention to the vulnerable, there will be, in the words of Ralf Dahrendorf, 'a high price in external protection, internal divisions and moral shame.' Since the new Eastern democracies are perhaps most vulnerable, they are the most urgent. It may be possible to restrain violence and the suppression of freedom within these countries by the European Convention on Human Rights, but that requires reading into national law.

It stems from the Council of Europe, founded in 1949, with its headquarters in Strasbourg to symbolise post-war reconciliation. Many of the Eastern democracies have applied for membership, and many parliamentarians already attend as invited guests. It can carry out, through the Committee of Ministers who are the Foreign Ministers of Member States, European Conventions, such as the Convention on Human Rights. This has done much to restrain illiberality.

But despite the promising development of the Council, there is ultimately a need for the European Community to include the new democracies fairly quickly. As Dahrendorf says, if we defer this issue 'we will indeed begin to become an ineffectual fortress, divided within and morally damaged by the betrayal of the liberal values in which we profess to believe.'[18] Similarly action on the growing unemployment within the Community is also required. Otherwise affluence becomes simply an expression of materialism.

So the relationship of justice to the emergence of the supranational Europe is the issue which theologians must address. Since the supra-national Europe is not yet fully come to birth, the values which it will embody are not yet clear. Justice remains an ideal in social relationships. The task is to move society towards justice, and the role of government is to mould society in this direction. It is therefore a question of approximation, and compromise, in the face of diverging interests. Even when situations appear intractable, there may be a possibility of action which uses 'fallen nature as in part the instrument for its own recovery.'[19] However in the past the nation-state could appeal both to the egoism and altruism of its citizens. Because there was no wider appeal beyond national egoism, it could become a force for evil, which was unchecked. Although groups represent and embody human sociability and sociality (the fundamental way we find our selves by relating to others), group egoism can become far more intense than individual egoism. That was the way nationalism ended in 1914.

Europe 1992 clearly shows that national self-assertion is no longer the only option in the final years of the twentieth century. What has transcended it is potentially a more universal entity, which is the Community. Here we return to Maritain's thought of the 'perfect society'. What remains the problem is what will check the egoism and selfishness of the Community itself. The question of compromise is not to be despised. As John Habgood, the Anglican Archbishop of York, has written:

'The notion that the will of God must somehow be unequivocal exercises a curious fascination over Christian minds. It leads to the suspicion that the ordinary human processes of argumentation and bargaining which result in compromises, represent a falling away of the ideal.' Habgood however is not arguing that discerning the will of God is the same as coming to a sensible compromise. Transcendence reminds us of human imperfection, and 'sets limits to the inadequacy claimed for all merely human responses.'[20]

This is perhaps the appropriate note to end this discussion of Europe 1992. God's infinite patience is held within his judgement, so there is a need, 'a sense of urgency to seize the creative moment when it comes. An acknowledgement that some otherwise messy compromises may nevertheless be faithful, can help to reduce guilt and recrimination.'[21]

'Europe' is in formation as a set of values, ideals and aspirations. The Maastricht Treaty is indeed a compromise, and it reflects both the conflicts of politicians and the uncertainty of how easily the old idea of the nation-state can be let go, to slip into history along with feudalism and the Holy Roman Empire. There is a real sense of urgency in Eastern Europe, and not much less in the Third World. Barriers, once erected, are not easily removed.

What then should be the role which the Churches should play? I have argued that after Maastricht the issues are those of justice and supra-nationalism, and that as the new Europe comes into being the values which it will hold depend on the decisions being taken now. And that, in turn, leads back to the dual recognition both of urgency and willingness to compromise. But that is for politicians. What should the Churches do?

In part they have responded through a series of well-informed briefings, pressure groups and conferences. Such bodies as the European Ecumenical Commission for Church and Society (EECCS) in Strasbroug and Brussels, the European Ecumenical Organisation for Development

(EECOD), the Churches Committee on Migrant Workers in Europe (CCME) do excellent work in providing information for Christians concerned about such issues. So too do conferences such as Malvern, England 1991, or the Monteforte, S. Italy conference of 1990. Both have published their papers.[22]

Ultimately however the theological issues must be addressed. In 1860 R. Cobden, an English MP who was a pacifist and an Anglican, negotiated a free trade treaty with France. He commended it on grounds that morality and culture, working through free trade, could draw together the nations into an eternal peace, beyond the antagonism of race, creed or language. We look back where this article began with the liberal Protestant vision of the unity of religion and human culture in harmonious nationalism. That was the vision of 1860. What similar vision can or should the Churches offer now?

Christian theology has been committed to a positive view of the non-Christian world after Vatican II 'with a generosity which would have astonished many missionaries and their supporters in past generations.'[23] There is a strong tension here between claims to finality about the work of God in Christ, and the wish to affirm the goodness and truth of non-Christian religions. Can non-Christian religions be affirmed as true, but not final, while Christianity is still understood as having a unique and irreducible insight into the nature of God's ways with humanity? The resolution of this question turns on the way in which the inner dynamic of Christian faith is held to be the love of God which is prior to any human action at all. That love is shown uniquely in Christ.

The uniqueness of Christianity means that claims about personhood, values and freedom will continue to be made by the Churches. Alongside the Christian commitment to personal evangelism, the Churches continue to witness to social values, relationships and truth. The way they will witness to this must in the Europe of the 1990s take account of the pluralism and diversity of European society, but it is a claim that will continue to be made. There will be no identity of purpose in the multitude of Europe's cultures. Yet the affirmation of human dignity and freedom, restated in terms meaningful to Europe in the 1990s, is the logical outcome of the Churches shared belief in the incarnation of Jesus Christ.

Conclusion

Religion and nationalism have been closely interwoven in the last century. This paper has not concentrated on the current, specific issues of employment, migration, trade or aid. These issues matter, but I have tried to take a longer view. Religion, and especially Christian theology, was a powerful force in developing what was felt to be a benign development of nationalism and culture before 1914. Since we do treasure the cultural roots of our present society, and these do take very different forms in different ethnic groups, liberal Protestantism was partly correct in affirming the growth of national cultures, as good in themselves. What was wrong was their failure to understand the demonic egoism which this brought. It is at least arguable that Barth's reaction against liberal Protestantism was, as Pannenberg believes, an overreaction: theology and culture ceased to be in dialogue, however understandable Barth's reaction may have been. The 1950s and 1960s saw the emergence of a Roman Catholic attempt to provide some theological markers for a more international order, while Protestants were more concerned to limit the pretensions of the nation-state (Dunstan, Thielicke). Yet Maastricht is neither supra-national nor a reaffirmation of nationalism. It is a confused Europe which is now emerging, where the need for justice (and compromise in the search for justice, so we do not remain content with high – sounding ideals) is all-important. The Churches are beyond doubt struggling with this change. On the one hand, there is the proper and good development of pressure-groups, information briefings, etc. On the other hand, there is the need to develope a Christian theology which can affirm the whole, created world and the multitude of faiths, while remaining faithful to the uniqueness of Christ. Bodies such as International Consultancy on Religion, Education and Culture, which work on the relationship of each world faith to the care of the creation and the environment, are important indications of the way forward. What is needed is a Christian ethic of justice and freedom, which can express the loyalty and allegiance its citizens will express in the new Europe, while remaining open to the world, especially the vulnerable of the world.[24] Such an ethic will need to turn to a deepened understanding of Catholicity, in an exchatological sence, as a hope for the world which is rooted in Christ. The task of developing such an ethic for the new Europe is perhaps the main challenge to the European Churches in the 1990s.

Notes

1. T.L. Knutsen, *The History of International Relations Theory*, Manchester University Press, Manchester, 1992.
2. Edmund Wilson, *To the Finland Station*, W.H. Allen, London, 1940 is the classic account of nationalism and socialism from Michelet to Lenin.
3. F.R. Dulles, *America's Rise to World Power 1898-1917*, Harper Torchbooks, New York, 1954; Henry F. May, *The End of American Innocence 1912-1917*, Jonathan Cape, London, 1960; William Appleman Williams, *The Roots of the Modern American Empire*, Anthony Bland, London, 1970.
4. G. Barraclough, *An Introduction to Contemporary History*, Penguin, London, 1967.
5. P. Hefner, *Faith and the Vitalities of History* (on Ritschl), New York, 1966.
6. T.A. Langford, *In Search of Foundations: English Theology 1900-1920*, Abingdon Press, New York, 1969; G. Wayne Glick, *The Reality of Christianity* (on A. von Harnarck), New York, 1967.
7. Para 1: 'crafty agitators are intent on making use of these differences of opinion to pervert men's judgments and stir up the people to revolt.' There is an indispensable new guide to nineteenth century Roman Catholic social thought in Paul Misner, *Social Catholicism in Europe*, Crossroad, New York, 1991.

8. Theologically, S. Bulgakov also attacked the sterility of liberal Protestantism. See ed. J. Pain and N. Zernor *A Bulgakov Anthology*, especially the essay on Solovyov's Christian Nationalism (pp. 42-51), SPCK, London, 1976.
9. Cited in Anton Pelinka *Social Democratic Parties in Europe*, E.T. Praeger, New York, 1983. The quotation (on p. 152) is from A. Langer ed. *Katholizismus und freiheitlicher Sozialismus in Europe*, p. 124, Bachem Press, Cologne, 1965.
10. D. Thompson, *Europe Since Napoleon*, Penguin, London, 1970 for the relationship of art and nationalism in 1900-1920.
11. G. Dunstan, 'National Sovereignty: a Theological Perspective' in British Council of Churches: *Christians and the Common Market*, SCM, London, 1967.
12. Dunstan p. 126.
13. Chicago University Press, Chicago, 1951.
14. Maritain, pp. 198-204. There is an excellent discussion in T. Weber 'Theological Symbols of International Order' *Journal of Church and State*, Vol. 29, Winter, 1987
15. W. Pannenberg and R.J. Neuhaus, 'The Christian West?' in *First Things*, New York, November, 1990; W. Pannenberg, *Christianity in a Secularized World*, SCM, London, 1989.
16. H. Thielicke, *Theological Ethics*, Vol. 2 (Politics), J. Clarke, Cambridge ET, 1980.
17. The Malvern Papers 1991. The Hinksey Centre, Westminster College, Oxford, 1991. See especially Chapter 3, p. 9, *The Economic and Social History of Europe*. Andrew Britton's quote is from an unpublished paper written for that conference.
18. Article in the *Financial Times*, London, December 12th, 1991.
19. Alan Suggate, *William Temple and Christian Social Ethics Today*, p. 192, T. and T. Clark, Edinburgh, 1987.
20. J. Habgood, *Church and Nation in a Secular Age*, pp. 179-189, 'Theological Reflections on Compromise', DLT, London, 1983.
21. Habgood, p. 189.
22. The Malvern Papers (see note 17); West European Network, *The Other Side of 1992*, William Temple Foundation, Manchester, 1990; R. Preston, *Religion and the Ambiguities of Capitalism*, Ch. 8 'North/South: The Responsibilities of Affluence', SCM, London, 1991.
23. D. Edwards, *Christians in a New Europe*, Collins, London, 1990.
24. On the new Europe: Maurice Crouzet, *The European Renaissance Since 1945*, Thames and Hudson, London, 1970 is an excellent guide to European culture from 1945-1970, by a French civil servant; H. Kaelble, *A Social History of Western Europe 1880-1980*, ET Gill and Macmillan, Dublin, 1989; S. Hardings, D. Phillips and M. Fogarty, *Contrasting Values in Western Europe*, Macmillan, London, 1986, is the first report by the European Value Systems Study Group.

6. The Spiritual Foundations of the European Thinking of Denis de Rougemont[1]

BRUNO ACKERMANN

Denis de Rougemont was one of the most committed essaysists in 20th century European literary life. From the outset he felt a bond with the personalist movement, which was to lead him into 'spiritual rebellion' against the 'established disorder'. Central to his works as a writer and thinker is the concept of the individual as a person who is both free *and* responsible, and of an ethic of thought and of action directed towards a 'common human measure'. Founded on the Calvinistic principle of 'active pessimism', his thinking stressed the duty of the writer to express *hic et nunc* the 'contemporaneity' of the Word. Denis de Rougemont's militancy – a militancy which cannot be separated from the concept of commitment, and one which he proclaimed long before that of Jean-Paul Sartre – was totally in line with that form of revolutionary humanism which preaches 'the defence of the total man against anything which seeks to mechanise, to disqualify and to emasculate him of all spiritual and creative violence'. The Christian vision of mankind is one of the aspects of his work which all too often goes unnoticed. His writings, generally seen as the work of a writer and essayist, a militant European and an ecologist, are filled with standpoints and critical reflection on the human being as a person, on liberty and responsibility, on love, myths, cultural federalism, and Europe. They seek to offer a response to the confusion of the modern world, to the intellectual and spiritual crises of an epoch which has become alienated by the major collective mystiques.[2] The works which he began to publish in the 1930s invited readers to reflect on the position of Man in the world, and on the spiritual foundations of European civilisation. To be convinced of this, we need only read many of these texts in order to detect the prophetic impetus behind them and to see that this author was, in his way, a 'theologian of European unity' and, as such, of European federalism. A theologian! Perhaps a surprising word to describe this essayist of critical temperament, of independent – and indeed sometimes provocative – mind when he had, in fact, no formal theological training. The son of a minister, trained in theology through his paternal upbringing within a family circle open to the ideas of 'Social Christianity', Denis de Rougemont became acquainted with Protestantism through his reading of the works of the great Danish writer and father of Christian existentialism, Kierkegaard, and the writings of one of the most rigourous dogmatists of Protestant renewal, the dialectic theologian, Karl Barth. In the period between the wars, Denis de Rougemont's active presence within the young activist personalist movements growing up around the journals *Esprit* and *L'Ordre Nouveau* and his association with the circles led by Jacques Maritain, Nicholas Berdiaeff and others provided fruitful ground both for his theological education and his commitment to the intellectual struggle.

Much more than a theologian in the strict sense of the term, Denis de Rougemont was, rather, someone who interpreted the Word of God in a manner which was both free and rigourous, audacious and courageous, not within the churches but in the university, political, intellectual and literary spheres, and – first and foremost – in those contexts in which debate was more polemical and virulent. We mention this fact not with the aim of discrediting the work of those theologians involved in exegesis but simply to indicate the way and the extent to which Denis de Rougemont practised theology and to point to those who were his immediate partners in dialogue and his opponents – among them the most doctrinarian Marxists and fascists, and those politicians and rationalist philosophers who stood out against the message of the Gospel. For Denis de Rougemont, Christian Scripture was, first and foremost, a personal requirement, just as it was a spiritual requirement in order to understand the times, to interpret the march of history confronted by a profound crisis of values of civilisation, an intellectual demand in an effort to bring to the people of his day this illumination, this taste for adventure, this risk called for and demanded by the Christian faith in order to rebuild a world which would be ever more human and ever more just.

Denis de Rougemont wished to open up, and indeed to pursue a dialogue between two opposing realities: the spiritual and the political, in other words between faith, or Christian action, and human behaviour in the world. Such a dialogue is all too often complicated by doctrinal intransigeance on both sides and by the contradictions inherent to such a debate. Yet today we see that such a dialogue is all the more necessary – in the West and elsewhere – given the fact that the present state or 'de-Christianisation' of 'de-spiritualisation', the decline in human relationships and technical aggression of Nature as a whole have become realities within a world in which we see unprecedented confusion, or even dangerous wanderings, in the field of spiritual and ethical values. This is the root of the anxiety of modern man. André Malraux once said that the 21st century will be spiritual or it will be nothing. Denis de Rougemont was one of those who believed that the next century would be – and indeed must be – spiritual.

While in his first doctrinal writings Denis de Rougemont claimed to have 'a certain natural aversion' to politics, he then went on to specify that from the moment that

'... Politics become the art of governing Man then it is up to those who exercise policy to know Man, the conditions of his humanity, and the rules which must be obeyed in order to respect his raison d'être'.[3]

It was precisely because Denis de Rougemont, like many young intellectuals in the 1930s, was concerned about the destiny of the Person in the modern world, of the fate the ideologies held in store for human beings caught up in the stranglehold of totalitarian systems, systems which gave birth to a type of individual deprived of liberty and of responsibility, that he felt the need to serve the community, to define the pressing, urgent directions which European society must follow if it was to work for its own salvation and for the salvation of all mankind. He became involved in this struggle not for purely intellectual reasons but out of conviction, because of his calling. Given the deep crisis of values facing Western civilisation, the remedies put forward by politicians were too simplistic and too dangerous, because they all led to the cult of collective and totalitarian mystiques, engendered new and fatal passions (blind nationalism), and extolled various forms of idolatries (the world of money), idolatries to which Europeans, past and present, are still prey.

Already in 1934 he wrote: 'To believe in Man is to believe in a model which human beings can or should be able to equal, but what can be the value of any model which Man can imagine of himself?'.

No matter the nature of the value of any model, be it humanist, Marxist or even Christian, the value of such a model 'can only be relative, doomed from the outset to common degradation'.[4]

Hence his personal involvement in the 'misery of the century', this permanent and ever-new Christian requirement which forms the source and spring of all human action in the heart of public life; the affirmation of the paradox inherent to all true Christian living, of that act of faith born in the depths of despair and which, alone, makes mankind truly human; hence, too, what he himself referred to as his 'active pessimism' or this 'revolution without any illusions', his commitment, this necessary *service* which defines the attitude of Christians in politics; hence, finally, his attitude of humanity in making his own the governing maxim of William the Silent, that Calvinist maxim *par excellence: 'We need not hope to act, nor succeed in order to persevere'*.

A personalist and federalist doctrine

The personalist doctrine which, already in the 1930s, Denis de Rougemont developed to counter the nascent collective passions, and later the diversions, in the construction of Europe was his personal intellectual and spiritual response to the challenge of our own history. It is an act of resistance to the fate of the century. Likewise, immediately after the Second World War, in 1946, he took up this same personalist doctrine in the course of the first *Rencontres Internationales de Genève*, meetings which united voices such as, among others, those of Karl Jaspers and Georges Bernanos at a time in European history which saw the beginnings of the reconstruction of the Old Continent which had been devastated at all levels – material and political, moral and spiritual. On the one hand there was the model of American society, on the other the Soviet model. Two opposing concepts of the human condition, neither of which offered mankind the true values of liberty. The only remedy for this state of civilisation was the European spirit developed and trained by a long cultural tradition. The peculiarity of the European spirit is fruitful separation, the creative conflict which, down through its history, has shaped an exemplary type of being, 'a certain *meaning of life*, a certain *awareness* of that which is human'.[5] It is true that Denis de Rougemont was not the only artisan of this new impetus breathing through the European spirit. A great many other names ought to be mentioned, from Jean Monnet to Robert Schuman.

The specific contribution of Denis de Rougemont was, however, the fact that he breathed the spirit of the productive values of Christianity into European reconstruction, 'simply in the name of the most conscious and creative humanity of mankind',[6] and of enriching the European idea with *creative utopias* – and in this Denis de Rougemont does not mean *already-known* utopias conceived on the basis of contemporary realities and therefore limited by our prejudices, but rather utopias which, on the contrary, would be 'descriptions of an order to be established, a more coherent society, one which is better ordered for good'.[7] Open as he was to the dialogue between the different cultures and religions, Denis de Rougemont was much more concerned with defending spiritual values rather than those values which were simply Christian. For this essayist is one of those thinkers who, while remaining coherent, develops further in their theological thinking, enriching their reflection on the phenomenon of religion and their practice of the faith by using certain subversive research into avant-garde poetry and psychoanalytical works – particularly the theories of Carl Gustav Jung – while still seeking to up-date the traditional dogmas taught by the churches, the speculations of modern, scientific or esoteric gnosticisms or, yet again, the spiritual values which form the foundations of the religions of India, the East or the Arab world. He was aware of the profound movements stirring in Christian circles, he was attentive, too, to the growing sense of community within the European churches, and which, among both Catholics and Protestants, took the form of a liturgical renewal. The essential aspect of this awakening was the fact that it was an expression of the common concern to order human finalities towards an incarnation, in terms of a common language, which would offer the only possibility of recreating, and indeed of inventing if necessary, a responsible community.

On the threshold of his battle for Europe, Denis de Rougemont's Christian thinking played a leading role in the ecumenical movement, launched at the beginning of the 20th century and which was to gain in depth when confronted by the drama of war. It was an ecumenism which meant not only an awareness of the scandal of divisions, of the common responsibility of Christians in the world and the urgent need for the restoration of the unity of the Church, but above all an openness to a dialogue between all religious tendencies, among all the Christian churches not only at the religious level but on the far wider level of *culture*, defined, on the one hand, as 'that global whole of objectives recognised by a given community' and, on the other, as 'all those values which enable (a community) to work to achieve these ultimate goals and ends and which will guarantee the validity of such action'. To raise the issue of the spiritual bases of the European thinking of Denis de Rougemont is, therefore, to raise questions with regard to the ultimate aims chosen by European man and European civilisation; it means questioning the values on which our cultural community is founded; finally, it is to direct the struggle of the people of Europe towards a goal which equals the values and the goals for which they have freely opted and, above all, to create the political institutions which will enable people to find themselves once again in harmony with the world around them. In the book which was to form his testament, *L'Avenir est notre Affaire* (1977) (English title *The Future is Within Us*), Denis de

Rougemont reminds us of the three great symbolic issues of concern at the end of the 20th centry: the Economy, in the material field, Ecology, in the field of nature, and Ecumenism, in the spiritual domain. Now these three words all have their origin in the Greek word *oikos*, meaning house. It is, therefore, a question of our inhabiting the earth, and not of filling it with our boredom with life or of peopling it with our internal disorders or pointless political blah-blah.

Given the extent and the depth of the problems affecting, indeed haunting, our contemporary societies, problems which destroy the structure of our ways of life and of thinking, the works of Denis de Rougemont provide an answer by situating the issues at stake today in terms of two fundamental concepts. On the one hand, the concept of the 'Person, free *and* responsible', and on the other, of a political system which is capable of respecting and bringing about this elevated concept of mankind: federalism presented as the absolute antithesis to the destructive dogma of the Nation-State. It is not a question of building new systems or of reconciling existing systems within a median synthesis, rather it is one of promoting, first and foremost, attitudes which are not only linked and interlinked but are revolutionary in the extreme, and new forms of action: the attitudes of personalism and of federalism. Having laid this corner stone, European Man's ideal and concrete route opens up naturally. It is a question of discovering and rediscovering the future, of converting human actions in the light and in the name of true and well-defined ultimate goals. What must be our starting point? What is our goal? Our starting point is the Person and the individual Person is – resolutely – our goal.

The Person and the calling

At the source of Denis de Rougemont's thinking lies the Person, the Person who is *human*, free *and* responsible, the basic nucleus of any living community. But who is this Person? As he looked for the meaning of Western mankind's search, Denis de Rougemont, in *Man's Western Quest*, reminds us of the path it has followed: 'Greek dialectic and Roman jurisprudence, on being catalysed by the Christian discipline, proferred the decisive word'.[8] It was thanks to the Greeks that the individual first acquired his measure as an individual. Having broken with the sacred order of the tribe or the clan he became this free *and* responsible Person, illustrated in Socrates' famous words: 'Know thyself'. Man becomes aware of his existence as an individual and frees himself from obscure forces. Under the Roman Empire we see the emergence of the concept of man as citizen, a human being defined by his social and juridical bonds which bind him, and make him subject to the laws of the City, the community. To interpret it symbolically, it is the triumph of the State, the triumph of the collective over the individual. The Judeo-Christian revolution, or Gospel, adds a third realm of values to this ethic, fitting into and based upon Greek wisdom and the Roman dogma of the all powerful State: the love of one's neighbour and the meaning of sacrifice. A new society comes into being: The Church which returns to Man his human dignity as a person as well as his active role within the community. The Church Fathers express this new reality of the Person in terms of the dogma of the Trinity which

'transports into God himself the paradox of the One and of the Many, whereas the Incarnation is the extreme expression of the coexistence of contraries, the unthinkable definition of the Person of Jesus Christ as "both true God and true man" '.[9]

Hence Man is defined by his transcendent vocation, and in the light of his conversion – this is the Christian meaning of the word 'revolution' – the Gospel commands him to love his neighbour. Thus the Person is bound to the community, but at the same time he is linked to transcendence.

As far as the sacred dogmas of the collective were concerned, Renaissance man went through a volte-face and claimed the right to free examination of everything and to free scientific experiment. Faced with this return to the paganism of the Greeks, the Reformation proclaimed the right and the duties of the Christian Person and restored man's obedience to the Word of God. While Calvin may not have added anything to the reality of the Christian being, he did contribute an essential specificity to the definition of the Person: the specific vocation of each and every human being,
'for the role which God attributes to a human being, distinguishes and isolates that human being, but at the same time it brings him into communication with his neighbour, thus *the dignity of each individual is guaranteed not by the simple fact that he exists*, physically, but by the fact that he can incarnate a specific desire on the part of God'.[10]

Thus, in the view of Denis de Rougemont, the Person is not an abstract value. Nor is this Person any longer an individual isolated within the anonymous mass of the people, or someone cut off from the world, devoid of aims, because such a vision of mankind bears within it a supreme consequence: the absolute power of the State, totalitarianism, and this the history of the 20th century has demonstrated only too well. The Person is a paradoxical reality, a human and spiritual entity endowed with a *creative calling* which is the foundation of any human community. Calling, as defined by Denis de Rougemont, is not 'a human choice (...) It is a call, a mission entrusted to a human being, – a word spoken to him by God'.[11]

It means being, at one and the same time, a solitary human being, and a human being in solidarity (in the words of Victor Hugo as quoted by Albert Camus), one who is distinct yet in relationship, autonomous yet a participant, one who is defined by a vocation which sets him apart but which, at the same time, calls him to serve the community. He is someone who not only obeys but who, above all, responds to the orders of the Divinity through concrete actions. He is the paradoxical man, the man ever linked 'to the world but not of the world', the man who lives 'in sin, but as one who has received the promise of being saved from the power of sin'.[12] In other words, the individual is a spiritual reality whose essential dimension forms part of that concrete and beneficent relationship which the Gospel refers to as the love of one's neighbour. Finally, the Person is the Incarnation *par excellence* of the Western quest for a living and creative equilibrium. For the personalist philosopher of the 20th century, it is above all 'the discovery not of the "I" but of the "Thou". The discovery of the concrete existence expressed by the pronoun "thou" '.[13]

If the Romanticism of the previous century led people to absolutise the 'me' and opened up infinite horizons, the 20th century, on the contrary, raised questions with regard to the need for the presence of 'the other'. Nicholas Berdiaeff wrote: 'Romanticism is not personalist, because the "I" becomes lost, becomes dissolved, in cosmic infinity".[14] In a remarkable book, *Ich und Du*, Martin Buber, the Jewish philosopher, for his part, presented the primal relationship of the I and the Thou in terms of the relationship between man and God, that relationship of which the Bible speaks. For Denis de Rougemont, this fundamental discovery of the neighbour, from the moment he confronts and questions us, is the foundation of the true community. The expression of the most elementary human community is brought to its realisa-

tion and finds its fulfilment in the couple, a mutual creation of two Persons in respect the one for the other. This was a theme which Denis de Rougemont was to develop and work out in the successive versions of his book *L'Amour et l'Occident*. Inversely, the true community, if it is, first and foremost, a means to enable Persons to find concrete fulfilment, is the place *par excellence*, where they can experience liberty, can take up their responsibilities and choose their destiny. But becoming a person in the fullest sense of the word is not the creative act of man alone:
'Man, as man, is indeed a creator, but he is a created creator, an obedient director, and his limits are those of personal incarnation. This is his order and his reality and the place of his redemption'.[15]
We need only remind ourselves that the Trinity[16] represented the major problem of the great Ecumenical Councils of the 4th and 5th centuries when they met in Nicea, Constantinople, Ephesus and Chalcedon. How, indeed, can we define and distinguish the three functions or divine relationships within a single God, the Father as the Creator, the Son as the Redeemer, and the Holy Spirit as Liberator, without sacrificing the divine unity or the diversity of the roles? The Nicean Fathers used the term 'person'.

'It is, above all, the definition of the Second Person of the Trinity, the Son, which was to form the Christian concept of man. By stating that they confessed Jesus Christ as "true God and true man" at one and the same time, the Fathers of the Council of Chalcedon established the first model which enables us to reflect, as a whole, on the antinomic realities, which in logic are mutually exclusive but which, de facto, coexist (...).'[17]

In formulating this thesis, the Councils gave their blessing to the important concept of creative antagonism first conceived by Heraclitus. In other words, the creation of a tension between two antinomic and complementary beings which must 'co-exist', without confusion, separation or subordination. It is on the basis of this concept of a God who is 'truly God and truly man' that Denis de Rougemont founds his Christian vision of man. He also finds support in Karl Barth's interpretation of the Trinitarian God.[18] This is the origin of his concept of the human person endowed with a two-fold vocation: temporal, on the one hand, vis-à-vis his 'neighbour' in the community which is the Church, spiritual on the other, vis-à-vis his God. Hence, too, the origins of his concept of Time and of History and of the Western Adventure. As a historian, philosopher and theologian, Denis de Rougemont became the interpreter of the major religious and metaphysical options of the great ecumenical Councils and has made their message relevant for our modern world. Man's fundamental conquest is a conquest of liberty, in other words, the power which man assumes over himself rather than over others. Adopting the conclusions which Mircea Eliade arrived at in *Le Mythe de l'Éternel Retour*, Denis de Rougemont turns to a philosophy of liberty which does not rule out God:

'The person is the essential work of each individual, and consists of finding one's own path and of experiencing one's own unprecedented adventure. For each person is born of something which has never existed before, which is unlike anything else, a growing of chromosomes which are themselves without precedent (...) Everyone of us is therefore the point of departure of a specific path towards the Goal which is calling us, no matter whether we call him God, the Absolute, Truth or Happiness. The Supreme Goal is the same for all, but in order to reach it, we must all create our own path, and blaze our own trail.'[19]

The path chosen by Denis de Rougemont, both in his writings and in his militant struggles, is expressed in the search for an original path which can save that civilisation of which he, on both the spiritual and the intellectual levels, is the clear-minded heir. The deep political troubles eating away at the roots of European civilisation call for the re-establishment of an order of values. With regard to the construction of Europe, the only possible path is that of federalism:

'Concretely (...) federalism means the autonomy of the Regions plus the computers, i.e. the respect of that which exists and of its infinite complexities which have finally been rendered possible by modern technology'.[20]
In other words, the federal union of Europe, not the enforced unification into one centralised and bureaucratic Nation-State leading to the decline of personal and community-based links; a free union within diversity, a living union of all the available forces founded on

'a vast complex of tensions, and thus of an on-going search for an equilibrium which is constantly called into question, and hitherto unknown discoveries raising ever new problems – in one word: an Adventure'.[21]

Federalism, a specifically European form of political thinking, is not merely a political system organised wittingly; it is, in the first place, a method, an art of *creating* a new civic space by safeguarding different and living values. Any political regime which claims to be federalist must, at least, respect the three founding principles: unity, or the desire for union, the real diversity of the communities, and the pact entered into voluntarily. While the first two elements, in logical terms, are opposites, they are nevertheless valid and vital: it is the tension, the interaction, which is created between them – and not their synthesis (in Hegelian terms) –

which constitutes the pact which can create the dynamism required for this federation, and which will therefore guarantee the solidarity of the members and protect their liberty. Yet again, while the *federalist problem* may be that of the creative confrontation of two opposing human realities, the federalist solution is a search for a creative and constantly active equilibrium. Basically, federalist thinking is founded on an adventurous dialectic, in other words, one which opens the road to new values.

The Ethics and the Politics of the Person

For Denis de Rougemont, a doctrine of the Person implies both an ethical and a political system: the *ethics of the person* arising from a vocation received and obeyed, in other words, one which is exercised within the community, and the *politics of the person*, resulting from the aims and ultimate goals which a political community plans to achieve, and from the conditions within which it is formed and functions.

The *Ethics of the Person,* as defined by Denis de Rougemont, is won through the exercise of a number of 'virtues'. The first of these is realism, which means dealing with the real problems, and the real dilemmas posed by any form of community life, rather the the supposed ones. The second quality is violence, not brutality or vulgar passion, but rather spiritual violence, the violence of the creative spirit, because 'every creative act violates a given situation (...), it contains a real threat to the person who dares to do it'.[22] The third quality is authority, the affirmation of a new authority which does not represent power but which is spiritual in essence, it is concrete, it represents the 'inseparability of thinking and of the risks it involves', manifested through the 'sense of the immediate grasped by the mind'[23] over concrete situations. The fourth quality: the taste for risk which alone commits human beings to become involved in real life and, in this way, testifies to the presence of reality and gives thinking its raison d'être. The fifth quality is originality, i.e. an act possessing true innovation in the life of the individual. The sixth quality, asceticism of expression, means restoring to speech, language, words and ideas their capacity to order and affect the concrete aspects of life:

'Ideally, we should make words dangerous, I would even say, unbearable, joyously and actively unbearable. To the benifit of silence on the part of the garrulous and action on the part of those who think'.[24]

The seventh quality is creative imagination, as opposed to imitation, which is something sterile, and to escape, which leads nowhere. The eighth and last quality is that of style, by this we mean the style inherent to the Person called to a commitment and an involvement which is driven by the desire to reach a goal. These qualities define the Person and enable him to act in a valid and on-going manner. They give the Person a density, a depth, a constant realness, and provide the deepest sources of his action within the community. In short, they bring man back to his origins and commit him to true ultimate goals.

According to Denis de Rougemont, the *Politique de la Personne* is represented by the Person's concrete commitments towards the community and all those actions which work together to bring about the creation of a true community. In this, politics, in the highest sense of the term, represents 'the art of creating a City in which every person can have an opportunity to be truly human'. In other words, it is the 'putting into practice of an ideal'.[25] Thus the politics of the individual calls for a two-fold approach: on the one hand an elevated concept of man, or an ideal, and, on the other, practical, ordered measures to bring about the achievement of this ideal. Federalism is the political expression of this personalist doctrine. Henceforth the construction of a federation is founded upon six basic principles: '(the) rejection of any idea of an *organising hegemony*'; (the) 'rejection of any idea of a system', in other words, of any form of ideological imperalism which, by definition, can only serve to destroy cultural and intellectual diversity; the recognition of and respect for minorities; the safeguarding of 'inherent qualities' (customs, laws, cultures) of each member of the federation; 'a love of the cultural, psychological and even economic complexities', a basic condition for the free exercise of liberties as opposed to the brutal and centralising simplism of totalitarian regimes; finally, a federation is built up 'not from the centre by governments', but *'from neighbour to neighbour, through individuals and groups'*.[26] This last principle is of capital importance for the future of European culture and society, because it forms the basis of the principle of personal responsibility incumbent upon each and every individual in the construction of Europe. A federal Europe worthy of the name can only be built on the basis of the Person, of small living communities.

'Because just as we cannot arrive at that which is universal save through that which is particular, it is only through the Person that we can enter into community. There can be no community except among Persons. All the rest is isolation in promiscuity. (...) *For the true Society is nothing more than a dimension of the Person.*'[27]

We have already mentioned the major attention which Denis de Rougemont paid to the ecumenical movement immediately after the Second World War. Confronted by the anxieties of a diseased modern world, he laid the foundations for a global reflection on the future of our societies:

'Political and economic health I shall identify whith federalism; moral and civic health with personalism; religious health with ecumenicity'.

His thesis was the following:

'(...) the theology of ecumenicity implies a philosophy of the person, the implication of which is the policy of federalism'.[28]

For Denis de Rougemont, ecumenical theology was not a utopian synthesis of existing theologies nor a completely revolutionary doctrine which would do away with the traditional theologies nourished by the Western Christian tradition. The strength of ecumenism lies in its call to the Church Universal. Its principal characteristic is that it believes that

'the diversity of divine calling is not an imperfection of the union, but its very life'.

To this he adds a second element:

'the theology of ecumenicity does not aim at dismantling the existing orthodoxies within the various churches. On the contrary, its first effect is to strengthen them by making them more conscious of their real value, and precisely by this detour it hopes to attain a profounder communion of spirit',[29]

on condition that these orthodoxies remain open and obey God, the only Master, because

'A church which pretends to be self-sufficient and to possess its own principle of unity, a church which tends to close itself from above in order the better to assure its human cohesion, at once becomes isolated and generates schisms. Its attitude is thus doubly anti-ecumenical. Its will for uniformity opposes union. It transforms diversity into division'.[30]

The Unity and the Diversity

We can adopt the same principles when it comes to the political construction of Europe. They are set out in the formula defined by Heraclitus which forms the basis of the dialectic of our European history and the source of our civilisation: that 'those things which are tending apart are actually being brought together'. This, Denis de Rougemont expresses as 'Unity within diversity' or 'the paradox of the One and the Many'. Personalism is the basis of the free community of Persons. Ecumenism lays the basis for a central spiritual position which will bring about the unity of Christians and of the churches while respecting their denominational differences.

At the level of European politics, we find this same principle in the federalist approach expressed in the paradoxical motto of the Swiss confederation: 'One for all and all for one'. No matter the kind of situation confronting Man, be it personal, spiritual or political, this motto continues to be relevant to the future of our civilisation. Indeed, it is basic. Any true ethic or policy of the Person goes beyond individual egotism, something which not only divides Man within himself but divides Men among themselves and destroys any efforts towards dialogue with the other major groupings of civilisation. True ecumenism excludes the dissident and sectarian visions of certain forms of orthodoxy. Likewise, a centralising State exercising absolute power over the members of which it is made up. True community is always born out of the smallest unit and out of respect for that unit. In turn, that community must respect the diversity of the nuclear groups represented, at various levels and in diverse measures or dimensions, by the Person, the couple, the family, the parish, the political constituency, the region, the federation. One of the key problems of the construction of Europe is that of the *dimension* of these areas which will make it possible for Persons to play a practical role in the life of the community. At the European level the region, which is diametrically opposed to the centralising concept of the Nation-State, may well represent one of the central realities of the future of Europe. This region is not defined by its geographical frontiers but rather by the extent of its influence, the convergence of interests, its ability to deal with city business, or of a group of municipalities, its ability to set up real *public services*, and to manage its own affairs. In short, a region is defined by a series of combined dynamisms and by their various consequences:

'(...) in the world of the regions, the liberty of the Person and the effectiveness of his action will be safeguarded by the opportunity of relating to and offering allegiance to groupings which will differ both in their nature, their role and their dimensions'.[31]

Just as the concept of the human person summons up the idea of community, the concept of a 'region', one which is autonomous with regard to action, options and political decisions, summons up that of European federation which alone can guarantee, indeed give legitimacy to, the autonomy of those regional units which compose it. *Autonomy*, does not mean *self-sufficiency*, something which would make any union or any trade with the outside world quite impossible. The Europe of the out-dated national myths thus discovers the Europe of the reality, a Europe woven from existing cultural and ethnic diversities, a vibrant Europe founded on a creative equilibrium and a fruitful management of differences. Plurality of relationships, and the fruitful tension which inspires them is the very principle of any human community, of any federation be it civic or political, spiritual or religious.

'(...) ecumenicity, personalism, and federalism are different aspects of one and the same spiritual attitude. They spring from one another and are interdependent. They have the same structures and the same ambitions. To the notion of rigid unity they unitedly oppose one of communion'.[32]

Federalism is but the direct expression, on the institutional level, of the relationships between Persons and the community. Once this link between the Person and the community has been established it is true that this relationship cannot gain meaning until we raise the issue of the ultimate goals. All of Denis de Rougemont's writings are based on this search for the 'ultimate meaning' of our lives, our thinking and of our actions. In a work published in 1936, and entitled *Penser avec les mains*, he reported on the status of 20th century culture which he claimed was irresponsible because it had no wish to become involved in the life of the community, and he – quite rightly – reminded readers that Man should think in actions, 'in the power of action', because any thinking only becomes effective once it is translated into action and brings about concrete results within the Person.

The choice of ultimate goals

What is the meaning of our lives? Modern man has created a world which, at one and the same time, threatens both his personal freedom, his spiritual freedom and his political liberty. The modern world, submerged as it is in a crisis hitherto unknown in the course of human history, is endangering not only the survival of Man, seen in his existential and personal context, but Man as the representative of the whole human species. This is the moment and the era of utter danger. Jean Bernard recently wrote that the 'Respect of the Person is a fundamental duty'.[33] The most urgent task facing mankind at the end of the 20th century is to define new human duties. In responding to this challenge, Man, for the first time in history, finds himself confronted by a choice between two deeply opposing situations: Power (collective, industrial, military, etc.), or Liberty (of the Person), both of which have their place in the history of Western thought. On the one hand we have a tendency which, beginning with Parmenides and Plato was gradually developed by Pierre du Bois, Machiavelli, Hobbes, Bodin, the Jacobins and Marx and resulted in the totalitarianisms of the 20th century. On the other, we find, in the front line, Heraclitus and Aristotle, Dante, Calvin, Althusius, Rousseau, Tocqueville, and Proudhon, whose ideas find their extensions in the theses of the federalists. The first concept calls for a limitation of thinking and for rationalism, and gives pride of place to the State; the second family of minds encourages a dialectic of thinking and gives precedence to the Person, the citizen. Denis de Rougemont's diagnosis of the crisis of the 20th century is unambiguous: it is the obsession with Power which is the real cause of all our moral and spiritual, social and cultural, political and economic crises; it is this obsession which is at the root of the systematic destruction of our Earth and of its resources. This lust for Power, cultivated and codified by the Nation-States, is a *catastrophic utopia*, which can only destroy values. In a Europe which, for decades, and in the light of the lessons of history, has tried to build a model of society based upon a better understanding between peoples, the temptations of nationalism and the crises of identity are both resurgent and dangerous phenomena. Given the difficulties inherent to the establishment of a community-based ideal, founded on respect for the Person, Europeans can safeguard themselves against their inherent weaknesses and temptations by formulating policies founded on values other than those which, to date, have unleashed two murderous wars. As our starting point, we must once again take Man in his reality and spiritual goals, says Denis de Rougemont, as well as the liberty of Persons, all of which summon up *creative utopias*, for it is these which engender responsibility and therefore liberty. The choice of European goals, which are also the common goals of all humanity, cannot be established unless Man gives new consideration to the issue of values:

'For European Man, whether he realises it or not, the Person is the absolute point of reference'.[34]

No longer is it the Nation or nationalist values or any form of the State which would stifle personal values, or political institutions which would deprive the Person of his rights or prevent him from exercising his duties in accordance with his conscience in due respect of his fellow-man. Power or Liberty? This is the choice confronting Western Man at the end of the 20th century. Hence the urgent need to redefine the goals of our societies, to establish a policy for our immediate future, and a society 'worthy of mankind' in which those liberties, guaranteed by the exercise of concrete responsibilities, can find expression, and finally to redefine new civic spaces, all kinds of communities in which people can share in the decisions directly affecting their future. In other words, solutions are not a new doctrine. The European mission *par excellence* is to define an ethic, i.e. a *praxis*. For Denis de Rougemont it is

'all those means which dictate a goal in order that we may achieve it. Only the end justifies the means, on condition that the end, in itself, is just, and that the means truly lead to the goal'.[35]

The ethic of federalism which Denis de Rougemont set out to define is founded on a series of virtues, all of which are complementary, all active, and all living in a reciprocal and creative tension.

The first quality is tolerance, in other words, an acceptance of otherness, of the infinite diversity of individuals and communities, of cultures and of religions. This can bring about solidarity and the recognition of the other person, my semblance and my neighbour. The quality of tolerance engenders what Denis de Rougemont calls the 'solidarity of the solitary'. The second quality is 'the courage, but also the duty, to be oneself'. Since each Person is unique and endowed with a personal calling, part of his task, his duty and his courage is to create his own path. Denis de Rougemont makes explicit reference to the words of the Psalm: 'Thy Word is a lamp *unto my feet*, and a light *unto my path*' (Psalm CXIX, 105). The third quality is a love of complexity, because any desire for simplification, for (political) unification inevitably leads to war and the establishment of a totalitarian system. The fourth quality is 'respect for that which is real' which means today, at the end of the 20th century, respect for 'the conditions necessary for humanity's survival'. In the political sphere it means the respect and recognition of cultural units, i.e. spaces where Man can make himself heard and take part freely in the decisions directly affecting his future and his destiny. The fifth quality is 'the sense of paradox' taught in the Gospels, which means that the smallest political and human entities are the least vulnerable and the most effective, and that 'respect for diversity is the precondition for any true Union'. Finally, the sixth quality: 'Humour' which is one form of the spirit of tolerance, 'in that it seeks to disarm violence'. Denis de Rougemont wrote that neither the Devil nor totalitarian systems can put up with a sense of humour:

'It is the sense of humour which saves men living in a democratic State'.[36]

Clearly these basic qualities of a federalist ethic are, in the first place, spiritual. They found our future, and establish new energies on the political, moral, social, religious and cultural levels. These qualities maintain intact our creative liberties, they guarantee the Person's spiritual life and, finally, they enable each and every person to fulfil his or her specific calling within the community. Having said this, is that Swiss federalism to which Denis de Rougemont often turned in founding his vision of a federalist Europe still a relevant model accepted by Europeans as a whole? It is clear that Denis de Rougemont's federalist vision assumes a political maturity which some European peoples may not yet have achieved. Are we not seeing, today, the resurgence of a certain old political disease, that of nationalism? Is it not the duty of Europe, today as in the past, to combat this fatal obstacle to the construction of Europe?

'(...) The Goal of the whole of human history, as viewed in the Christian perspective, is (...) the community of persons, set free and set in relation by virtue of faith'.[37]

If this is not the ultimate aim of our history and of our societies then we must reflect on this terrible question in the shape of an avowal: are we so frightened of being free? The sense of paradox and intellectual courage and audacity were the qualities characteristic of Denis de Rougemont. Should they not also by the qualities of Europeans at the dawn of a new millennium? In *The Future is Within Us*, Denis de Rougemont writes:

'The decadence of a society begins when people ask: *What is going to happen*, instead of asking themselves: *What can I do?*

Strangely enough there is only one possible answer to these two questions and it is: *Yourself*. For what happens depends on what we are: things will go from bad to worse if we remain as bad as we are, and some good will result if we become better, and become more obedient to our calling in society. Outside of this there can be no community (...) neither in Europe, nor can there be peace, nor a future with a human visage'.[38]

N.B. Works by Denis de Rougemont

The Heart of Europe, New York, Duell, Sloan and Pearce, 1941
Talk of the Devil, London, Eyre and Spottswode, 1945
The Last Trump, New York, Doubleday and Co., 1947
Passion and Society, London, Faber & Faber, 1956
Man's Western Quest, London/New York, Harper Brothers, 1957
The Myths of Love, London, Faber & Faber, 1963
The Christian Opportunity, New York, Holt, Rinehart & Winston, 1963
The Meaning of Europe, London, MacMillan, 1965
The Idea of Europea, London, MacMillan, 1966
State of the Union of Europe, Oxford/New York, Pergamon, 1979
The Future Is Within Us, Oxford/New York, Pergamon, 1983

Translated in English from French by Irene Bouman-Smith

Notes

1. Swiss writer and essayist (1906-1985). He studied at the Universities of Neuchâtel, Geneva and Vienna and in 1930 settled in Paris where he became literary editor of the 'Je Sers' publishing house. He was a co-founder of the reviews *Esprit, L'Ordre Nouveau*, and *Hic et Nunc* (of Barthian persuasion). He also

worked for the *Nouvelle Revue française*, and in 1932 produced the 'Cahier de revendications' of French youth. This was followed by a period of 'intellectual unemployment' (1933-1935) in the French provinces. Lecturer at the University of Frankfurt (1935-1936) and then principal editor of the *Nouveau Cahiers* (1937-1939). He returned to Switzerland in 1939 and was called up into the Swiss army and founded the *Ligue du Gothard*, one of the earliest manifestations of the spirit of European resistance. He also drew up its manifesto. Following a particularly acerbic article condemning Hitler's entry into Paris the Swiss authorities sent him to the United States. He became a professor at the Ecole Libre de Hautes Etudes in New York (1942) and thereafter editor at the Office of War Information of 'La Voix de l'Amérique parle aux Français' (1942-1943). Upon his return to Europe in 1947 he was active in the European federalist movements. He drafted the *Rapport culturel* at the Congress of Europe and the *Message final aux Européens* (The Hague 1948). In Geneva he founded and directed the Centre Européen de la Culture (1952-1966), out of which many European institutions were to grow, and presided over the Congrès pour la Liberté de la Culture (1952-1966). He was a founding member of the Groupe de Bellerive (1977), which instituted reflection into the direction being taken by industrial society. He was also a pioneer in writings dealing with the dangers of nuclear energy. Bibliography, cf. Denis de ROUGEMONT, *Inédits*, (extracts of lectures selected and presented by Jean Mantzouranis and François Saint-Ouen), Neuchâtel, La Barconnière, 1988, pp. 217-241.

2. For a global approach to Denis de Rougemont's works see *Du Personnalisme au fédéralisme européen*, Geneva, European Cultural Centre Publications, 1989, 316 p. and *Cadmos* (quarterly review of the European Cultural Centre), no. 33, Spring 1986.
3. *Politique de la Personne*, Paris, Je Sers, 1934, p. 20.
4. *Ibid.*, p. 24.
5. ***, *L'Esprit européen*, Neuchâtel, La Baconnière, 1947, p. 153.
6. *Ibid.*
7. *Inédits*, Neuchâtel, La Baconnière, 1988, p. 150.
8. *Man's Western Quest*, (1957), New York, Harper & Brothers, p. 38.
9. *Lettre ouverte aux Européens*, Paris, Albin Michel, 1970, p. 41.
10. 'Le protestantisme créateur de personnes', *Mission ou Démission de la Suisse*, Neuchâtel, La Baconnière, 1940, p. 32.
11. *Politique de la Personne*, *op. cit.*, p. 60.
12. *Ibid.*, pp. 88-89.
13. *Penser avec les mains*, Paris, Albin Michel, 1936, p. 234.
14. Nicholas BERDIAEFF, *Cinq méditations sur l'Existence*, Paris, Aubier, 1936, p. 106.
15. *Penser avec les mains*, *op. cit.*, pp. 248-249.
16. cf. Bernard LAURET and François REFOULE, *Introduction à la pratique de la théologie*, Paris, Cerf, 1986, vol. III.
17. 'La personne comme fondement des valeurs européennes', *op. cit.*, p. 6.
18. 'The Word of God is the revelation of God himself. For God reveals himself as Lord. With regard to the concept of revelation in Scripture, this means that God

himself, in his unalterable unity, but also in his unalterable diversity, is the revealer, revelation and that which is revealed', cf. Karl BARTH, *Dogmatics*, I, 1, 2, Paris, Labor, 1963, p. 1.

19. 'La personne comme fondement des valeurs européennes', see Deuxième Table Ronde du Conseil de l'Europe, 19 September 1957 (D.69.558), p. 7.
20. 'L'avenir du fédéralisme', in *La Revue de Paris*, September 1969, p. 8.
21. 'Les options fondamentales de l'Europe', in *Annuaire de l'Institut Universitaire d'Etudes Européennes*, Geneva, 1957.
22. *Penser avec les mains, op. cit.*, p. 207.
23. *Ibid.*, pp. 212-213.
24. *Ibid.*, p. 222.
25. 'A hauteur d'homme', in *Réforme*, 1 June, 1946.
26. *L'Europe en jeu*, Neuchâtel, La Baconnière, 1948, pp. 70-77.
27. *L'Avenir est notre affaire*, Paris, Stock, 1977, p. 234.
28. *The Christian Opportunity*, New York, Holt, Rinehart and Winston, 1963, pp. 142-143.
29. *Ibid.*, p. 144.
30. *Ibid.*, p. 145.
31. *Lettre ouverte aux Européens, op. cit.*, pp. 173-174.
32. *The Christian Opportunity, op. cit.*, p. 151.
33. *De la biologie à l'éthique*, Paris, Buchet-Chastel, 1990, p. 200.
34. 'La personne comme fondement des valeurs européennes', *op. cit.*, p. 5.
35. 'Notes pour une éthique du fédéralisme, in *Menschenrechte, Föderalismus, Demokratie, Festschrift zum 70. Geburtstag von Werner Kägi*, Zurich, Schulthess Verlag, 1979, p. 259.
36. *La Part du Diable (1942), The Devil's Share*, New York, Pantheon Books, 1944, p. 96.
37. *L'Aventure occidentale de l'homme (1957). Man's Western Quest, op. cit.*, p. 40.
38. *The Future is Within Us*, Oxford, New York, Pergamon, 1983.

7. Struggling for the Human Face of Europe*

H.M. DE LANGE

Introduction

On the fifth of November 1990 there was an unusual meeting in Brussels. That day the president of the European Community Jacques Delors spoke with representatives of Protestant and Anglican churches in Europe. Delors expressed his feelings regarding particular developments in the Community. His conclusion was: 'the EC lacks a heart and a soul'. Least of all very common language for a politician, but certainly reflecting an anxiety for the future of our continent.
This event immediately brings me back to a moment more than 30 years ago. At that time I read one of the most challenging speeches: the address of dr. M.M. Thomas held at the Ecumenical Youth Assembly in 1960. Under the title 'The European Churches of the World Today' he reminded the participants that the days of European expansion and dominance had come to an end. Asian and African nationalism – he said – today represent a new spirit of independence which will not accept anymore colonial or imperialist domination. MM also spoke of the emergence of America and Russia as the two big powers. This should not lead to apathy about world affairs and to dreams of the past history. On the contrary. I quote: 'Europe has a historical function to fulfill in world affairs, a vocation which will be humbler in terms of power, but nevertheless a vocation which may be no less significant in terms of service to humanity. And the main task of the European churches is to help Europe to discover

her new vocation in the world, the new pattern of her service to the world.'

During several decades Europeans discussed the question of 'the historical function' and the challenge of 'the new pattern of service to the world.' To evaluate whether the EC is a true answer to these questions one has to consider another part of MM's speech. I quote: 'Europe has had the tradition of a certain concern for men. I know the word humanist is suspect in Europe and means man's affirmation of his self-sufficiency. But it is a good word and may also be used to express the idea of a genuine concern for men as persons... I am speaking of that genuine humanism derives from the Christian Gospel which has always insisted that man is an end, not merely a means..., that the essential humanity of man can find fulfilment only if he is free to respond to the Word of God and live in a community of responsible persons.' In regard to these well-stated principles Europe always showed a split soul. During my life-time the cruelties of two ideologies were a betrayal. The result was that millions of people lost there lives and many other millions suffered under violence and oppression. It is my opinion that the colonial policies were another betrayal against the deepest intentions of the genuine humanism of which MM spoke in Lausanne 1960.

The foundation and the shaping of the European Community has to be considered an unfinished and incomplete reply to the fundamental goals and ends. In this article I shall explain the scope of the incompleteness especially regarding the adequacy of economic policies. First of all I shall sketch some outlines of the European Community itself and the present state of the so-called European Single Act. Looking backwards and looking into the nineties, I then will present some shortcomings and new challenges.

The European Community

The background of the Treaty of Rome which set up the European Community was the antagonism between France and Germany and the threat of the Sovjet-Union. The proposal to integrate the steel works of both countries – some years earlier – was the brilliant idea of Jean Monnet. With this proposal he satisfied French nationalism and brought back Germany in the conference-room. Monnet's proposals became the corner-stone for further economic cooperation of six, later nine, and now twelve countries. Within a couple of years there will be more – Austria and Sweden. I recall that almost all European countries had a similar economic history and traumatic experience. I refer to the depression of the thirties, which caused human despair, humiliation and poverty. This originated the swampy ground on which national socialism and fascism could grow and could undertake a demonic policy of aggression and murder. During the depression, national governments built up state regulations to protect their nations from economic calamities. That failed completely. The policies exacerbated the depression and one of the consequences was mass unemployment, destroying the lives of millions of people. After World War II a social security system was in part a response to this kind of calamity. Such social systems are still in the hands of national governments, because a common market in itself is not a guarantee against unemployment. And the current situation in the European Community mainly *is* a common market, combined with detailed regulations for international trade and for agriculture. The Community plans to complete the internal market by 1992 by removing barriers to the free circulation of goods, services, and means of production. The aim is to promote European specialization, strengthen competition and increase efficiency. In other words, growth, higher production, and higher consumption, wealth and welfare. Next to the common market, all the Member States have their own mixed economies, that is to say, economies in which industry is responsible for the total production, the direction of production, the varieties of products, etc., using a price and market mechanism. On the other hand, governments are manipulating these decisions on production by a vast variety of regulations on prices, incomes, taxation, subsidies etc. In each country the mixed economy has a different mixture and shape. One of the leading concepts in this development of more than 30 years is this idea of mixed economy, which can be discovered more clearly in the particular states than in the Community as a whole. This type of organization of the economy is a reply to the laissez-faire economy with its blindness for the imperfections and the limitations of the market. No doubt, there are several unsolved economic problems in these (national) mixed economies. It is my opinion that these shortcomings partly only can be solved by the Community itself (partly only on a global level). The main problem, however, is the transfer of *political* power to Brussels. That is the background of the struggle between the Commission and the Council of Ministers, in which the last mostly is the winner.

The mixed economy is an economic system, but one should recognise that is not identical with unchangeable and rigid. There is an ungoing debate on the 'mixed' itself, both in the Member-Countries as well as in the Community. The outcomes of these discussions depend on political views. Christian Democrats and Social Democrats represent two important political streams, which agree on the idea of the mixed economy. A new terminology is the so-called 'social market'. In regard to this idea it can be observed that Christian Democrats tend to the (too optimistic) view, that market-forces in itself give birth to a social (and environmental) policy and that Social Democrats have the opinion that to be social there always is a need for political action.

The reason for this action is the unequality in the economic process between individuals and groups, and the need to protect the interests of the whole.

In his article 'Reflections on the present economic situation from an ecumenical perspective' (published in *Reformed World*, June 1991) Julio de Santa Ana writes: 'European integration can be understood as an expression of *moral responsibility* (his italics), giving thrust to a new political will, which is leading Western European peoples to integration of their market by the end of 1992... To give priority to integration rather than to competition, to joint ventures rather than to antagonism, has been an impressive moral shift in European behavior. However, it must be noted that such reorientation took place within the system.' He adds: 'Changes were only introduced within this fundamental reality' of a price and market mechanism. My question is: what is wrong with this? A price and market mechanism does not have a smell of divinity. The question is: who has the power for change? And: is there a fundamental will for change? I agree that there was a new moral responsibility. Nevertheless, there was also a economic and political necessity to reorient. Of course the two motives were intertwined.
It is the credit we must give Jean Monnet that he had a 'nose' for the moment suprême and was able to shape necessities in political steps.
On the basis of the so-called Single European Act (SEA) the Community now is processing in a new stage, primarily the achievement of a European internal market, without suppressing barriers to the circulation of goods. An internal market with a stable growth rate, which should reduce the number of unemployed. The SEA is a series of amendments to the existing treaties. Included is the constant struggle to establish a monetary union and to implement a common regional and social policy. The SEA also mentioned the urgent

need of environmental protection as a component of the Community's policies. All these issues bring us to the next paragraph. Before doing so I want to make a few conclusions and to underline some of my views.

1. It would be a false conclusion that I am not willing to discuss the fundament of the present economic order. It is my opinion that steps in the direction of optimalization can be set by the development of new economic policies, both at the national level and at the European level. The same is true – of course – for the global level.

2. There is not only one concept of the mixed economy, but the Members of the Community economically have more in common than that there are differences. In each country of the Community government is playing a role in economic life. There is one particular power-bloc – in particular the Trans National Corporations whose influence is asking for political countervailing. Respect the Commission in Brussels is too weak.

3. The combination of common market (with a small beginning of a mixed economy) on the one hand, and well shaped mixed economies on the national scale on the other hand so far eliminated poverty to a large extend for the majority of the population. Standards of living have been improved, there is a big change in human welfare and education in comparison with our parents. There is also a complete change in life-style, generally spoken of as positive in economic terms. Not everyone profits, however, and a high price has to be paid. To these problems I come back in the next paragraph.

Shortcomings and challenges

I regret to say that the SEA is a weak document regarding present shortcomings and challenges. I shall summarize them in four short paragraphs.

A. Poverty in Europe

To banish poverty is one of the overruling ambitions of economists. There has been progress – as already mentioned – in the Member-States and sometimes even a feeling of triumphalism arose in the firm belief that we could succeed in banishing poverty altogether. New studies of the European Community, however, showing that at least 50 million people can be characterized as poor, have dampened these feelings of triumphalism considerably and made us more modest. Even if we accept that this poverty-problem in our countries is partly psychological, one has to accept that these feelings are very relevant for those engaged. The poverty in Europe is a relative one, compared to poverty in Asia, Africa, and Latin-America, but the deficiencies in many households, esp. in those of old people and in those of prolonged unemployment are considerable. The problem of poverty marks the disparities in the Community. There is not only a (slightly diminishing) disparity between the Northern countries and the Southern in the Community, there is also the unequality in the Member-States itself. In the last fifty years unequality was reduced in a number of countries. There is a great variety of opinions whether equality should be tolerable and whether the reduction of equality has to be seen as an essential condition of social consensus.

There is a Anti-Poverty Programme of the Community (about 40 projects). It is my impression that the urgency to promote this social dimension of the construction is felt stronger in Brussels itself than in the capitals of the twelve Members. The bureaucracies of the Twelve are not very willing to transfer financial power to the Brussels centre to widen and to deepen the programme. In most of the countries there is a fundamental lack of interest for their own poor.

B. Structural unemployment and Work

During the last decade the nature of economic growth has changed. Especially industrial investments can create more national product, but not more jobs. The banking system shows the same problems as the industrial sector. The mechanisation of the large administrative system brings down the total number of those employed.

For the majority of the people at the same time there is a downgrading mobility. For a minority there is upgrading. A Working Group of independent experts – set up by the Commission in the context of its studies on Medium-Term Economic Assessments – reported already in 1979: 'There is a widening gulf between the aspirations of a better educated, more cultured population and the reality of boring, repetitive tasks involving only a small part of a highly ordered process. The reward for this alienation, increasing material comfort, is increasingly inadequate or questioned, as the consumer society and economic growth are unfavourably compared with other values such as the quality of life, leisure, the right to live in one's home town.' It is no longer correct to accept blindly the well-stated words of John F. Kennedy (30 years ago!): 'A rising tide lifts all boats'. Economic progress now can be the cause of social marginalisation. Structural unemployment – both for men and women – is the feature of today's situation in almost all Member-Countries. Labour-problems have to be discussed in connection with so-called modern technology. This discussion can take place in our different countries, but policies only can be executed by the countries together. The SEA again is weak on this issue. It is my firm belief that churches bear a great responsibility to find a solution for the employment problem. Christian ethics for a great deal is based on a view of work itself. The idea was and is that work is an intrinsic and irreplacable part of human existence. Work not only is an economic necessity, but also a social value for almost everyone. We can not abandon work in our lives, but we should remind ourselves ànd society that work should not be identified with paid work only. To gain some self-realisation and respect, to have a relationship with others, to fulfill the idea 'work is inseparable from service to our fellow-men' (J.H. Oldham), we should reconsider the whole concept of work and not only the income-related part.

The instrument traditionally applied by governments to fight unemployment – stimulation of production – has lost its meaningfulness in Western society. The solution for structural unemployment primarily is not an economic one, but a cultural one and that exactly is the entrance for churches.

C. Environment in an integrated Europe

More and more people are aware that the old economic paradigms do not take into account ecological and resource limits and the physical sustainability of the economy. Stewardship is not in safe hands with those who are guided by the unqualified concept of growth. The draft document of the WCC 'A guide to economy as a matter of faith' says: 'There is a major link between environmental destruction and economic policies and it is in this field that we again can observe a major failure of prevailing political-economic models. Some of the dominant economic theories underlying these models are defective in the sense that they do not study the phenomenon of scarcity as such and that they assume that the needs of individuals are limited. Often they do not distinguish between need and greed, equate economic growth with development, limit the concept of value to market prices and market value, and regard ecological factors as 'externalities' which cannot be measured and fall outside the scope of basic economic theories.'

This statement is in line with the Seoul-documents, where it reads: 'The rich countries should accept a limit to growth so that resources can be made available for production aimed at fulfilling the international basic needs of all; all basic needs of a society and its people determine economic and political policies and not the economic values and interests of transnational corporations and international monetary agencies such as the international Monetary Fund and the World Bank.'

Option for the poor means more production to *them*, basic needs, but with a given *limited* environmental space, the industrialized countries confront a change in consumption patterns. The very successes of economic growth have not been achieved without costs. More and more we see these costs: destruction of beauty, dangers of pollution, exhaustion of resources. We have to start talking of 'justice between generations', because future generations now are threatened by the present generations and esp. by those who are rich.

The Brundtland definition of 'satisfying the needs of the present without compromising the needs of the future' is not very helpful. Most environmental destruction is the direct responsibility of industrialised countries, only a small proportion of whose production can be said to be related to 'needs'. The satisfaction of wants and desires is what drives Western economies and Brundtland says nothing about those. Neither does the European Single Act. The people of Europe has to think about a revised development-model, according to the basic principles mentioned in the beginning of this article. Urgent is to build up a public pressure in favour of policies safeguarding the environment for future generations, and as a habitat for other species too. The European Commission must accept the extension of its horizon to encompass environmental externalities associated with the production of raw materials, imported by EG countries, especially of agricultural goods originating in developing nations. On the other hand pesticides export-regulations are an item for concern at EC level.

We should be aware that many environmental problems have global ramifications. Here the question of sovereignty is at stake. We cannot solve 20th century problems with a framework of past centuries.

D. Responsibility for others

I mentioned already the paradox of the Brundtland-report. The paradox is that, although development is resource-utilising and therefore pressure on the sustainability of soils, water, forests, air, yet it is only through a process of development that we can achieve the balance which will save us. I indicated this process of development for Europe, at least the countries of the Community. Going that way can give us credibility by asking others to do the same. To be open for others is a Christian virtue. It is mostly hampered by a complacent short-term view of our interests. We know already for decades that mass-poverty, including world hunger is the striking phenomenon in other continents. From the point of view of the total number of poor people – 1.000 million and probably more within the next years – the world economic system and the national system appears to be a complete failure.

What jumps out at the eye is a political unwillingness to act. The responsibility for bold decisions cannot be pushed into the hands of the governments only. Public opinion – on the whole – is lukewarm, although there are many NGO's dealing with development, including church organisations. EG-policies regarding redistribution of political power and to make self-determination meaningful are weak. On the contrary, there is a continuation of an agricultural policy which in itself is a disaster for many developing countries and for millions of farmers. Furthermore there is a tendency to protect its own production (both agricultural and industrial). There is a fundamental lack of willingness to share power. The continuation of the debt-crisis is another example that shows that European countries are mainly dealing with their (short-sighted) interests. The Lomé-Treaty has to be renewed totally, in this sense that the wish in more and more African countries to develop their own model should be encouraged and be accepted, also if this has a delinking element regarding Western economies. European countries can stimulate this process by making bold proposals for the present debts and for the idea 'cash for green'. In other words: the demands in financial terms for the greening of production need a positive reply.

Final remarks

1. It could be of some interest to investigate whether Christian lay people are willing to sit together for thinking and designing a renewed model for the future development in Europe, considering (i) the limited environmental space, (ii) the option for the poor. The biblical justice-concept is the guide for such a design.
2. This study should include the re-assessment of the present welfare-state and social services. Here again some vital principles are at stake. The study should also include an outline for a World Public Sector, i.e. the first steps for the international shape of a welfare policy.
3. The study can be done under the auspices of the European Ecumenical Commission for Church and Society at Brussels, with the condition that participants of the Roman Catholic church and that lay people from the Eastern part of Europe should be invited to participate.
4. We should be aware of MM's admonition to 'search for new patterns of service to the world'. That means a reply to the 'call for the total transformation of unjust structures and patterns of behaviour' to which the Basel European Ecumenical Assembly invited us.

For whom and for what are we waiting?

Note

* A few paragraphs of this article are identical with my contribution to *Reformed World*, Volume 41, Number 6, June 1991, called 'Reflections on the Present economic situation from an Ecumenical Perspective'.

8. Will the Indian Outlast Europe?

MAARTJE VAN PUTTEN

The changes in Eastern Europe, the question of a proper political and governmental structure for Europe, which must be resolved this decade, and the search for a way out of the Balkan tragedy, all mean that the EC has plenty on its hands. One unintentional danger of this increasing pressure on the European political agenda may be that there is no time left to consider the problems of the 'South', to use a somewhat outmoded term. However, if we are unable to look at the role of Africa, Asia and Latin America in the worldwide current of events or to take them into consideration in our solutions to the major political problems of the day, there is a danger that the solutions now proposed will soon turn out to have been the wrong ones.

In other words, if we are unable to make the connection between problems such as the rapid deterioration of the environment and the growing division of the world into rich and poor, the rise of racism and fascism, the disintegration of states and the growing quest for cultural identity, the fear of a mass influx of refugees both from the South and the East, economic interdependence and the threat of recession, the problem of debt, or the marginalization of women and children, then no political solutions will be possible either. It would be simpler to answer each of those questions on its own, but their interdependence is in itself the greatest problem. In fact we have known this for a long time, since it was set out in the report 'Limits to Growth', published by the Club of Rome in 1972.

Without attempting a complete list, I would like to raise a number of problems which are on Europe's doorstep. These are the developments in Europe which will ultimately determine the face Europe shows to the Third World.

The attacks on the homes of asylum-seekers in Germany – as well as expressions of racism elsewhere in Europe – are a depressing sight. However, the real refugee problem lies not in Europe but in the Third World itself. The numbers of refugees applying to enter Europe pale into insignificance beside the millions of refugees received by the Third World countries themselves.

It is true that the migratory flow (surplus of immigrants over emigrants) into the EC rose sharply from 250.000 in 1987 to 675.000 in 1988, with the figure for 1990 estimated at something over 1 million. The case of Germany is particularly striking. Two thirds of the EC's total migratory surplus between 1985 and 1989 ended up in Germany. The people in question were mostly ethnic Germans from countries such as Poland, the Soviet Union and Romania (known in German as 'Aussiedler'). In addition, since the outbreak of war in the former Yugoslavia, Germany has taken further hundreds of thousands of refugees. No other EC Member State has yet shown such an open attitude.

According to the UNHCR, the United Nations' refugee organization, 60% of all asylum applications in Europe were made in Germany.[1] There are very few applications for asylum in Britain. Even more striking is the fact that the number of asylum seekers in France has actually fallen over the last two years. This coincided with the drafting of Europe's strictest laws on asylum. Why this panic in Europe?

Admittedly these figures say nothing about the number of illegal immigrants, for whom there are no statistics. However, the countries of Southern Europe seem to have taken the largest numbers of illegal immigrants over the past few years. In Spain their numbers are said to have doubled in a few years (mostly North Africans, Latin Americans and a remarkably large number of Filipinos). According to one of our Spanish colleagues, conditions in the Mediterranean are becoming reminiscent of Vietnam or the Rio Grande. Every day, more bodies are washed up on the beaches. In Italy, estimates as high as 1 million were, given last year for illegal immigrants from Ghana.

But why from Ghana particularly? Is not migration a structural, worldwide issue, a symptom of differences in development, wealth, economic structures (including debt), in short, a difference in life opportunities? If we accept that the net flow of money from the South to the North is still greater than the flow in the opposite direction, we should not be surprised that the same is true of the flow of people. As long as the EC is not prepared to solve the debt problem, what right have we to complain?

Let us take the example of Ghana with its debts estimated at US$3 billion in 1989.[2] This was the country where the World Bank first began its structural adjustments, taking the form of privatization, cuts in government bureaucracy and widespread unemployment. If there is any connection between these events, the next flood of refugees will be from Uganda, where 40,000 public servants were recently sacked in the capital within one month.

The figures are well known.[3] In 1991 the Third World's total debt fell by U$ billion to US$ 1,351 billion. Very little of this drop has been felt by Africa. In ten years, indebtedness in the sub-Saharan countries has risen from US$56 billion to US$174 billion, greater than the sum of their own gross national products. The African countries' creditors are mainly European governments and EC institutions.

In view of these developments, it is hard to understand why Europe does not already have a long-standing long-term policy in this area. Debts cancellation is a political act. Poland has been released from half of its debts as a reward for introducing a market economy. The same happened with Egypt for its cooperative attitude in the Gulf War. Clearly, Africa has little to offer us. One only needs to look at the flows of migrants to see how short-sighted this attitude is.

It is the changes in Eastern Europe which will most change Europe's attitude to the South. In the Netherlands the debate on shifting the development budget from the South to the East has been under way for some time. The same tendency has been noticeable in the rest of Europe, too. But the European Parliament, which has more power over EC spending than many people realize, has put a stop to this. It has taken the view that a new policy means new money: aid to Eastern Europe must not be at the expense of development aid.

However, an examination of the EC budget reveals that well-known items such as those for Asia and Latin America and for emergency aid have remained about the same, or risen slightly, while by comparison aid to Eastern Europe has risen sharply. Aid for Eastern Europe now constitutes 30% of the total development budget.

Though this idea may be hard for many to get used to, I am convinced that the only correct way forward is to link development aid to the South with that to the East. After all, what does the term 'developing country' mean nowadays?

Is it still possible to speak in these terms? Is the term 'the South' not now outmoded, as I suggested above? We should redefine our terms in accordance with the OECD Development Assistance Committee's standards. Take, for example, the average per capita GNP for Barbados, Portugal and Poland. In Barbados the figure is US$ 6,010, in Portugal US$ 3,650 and in Poland US$ 1,860[4]. The Uzbekistan, Turkmenistan, Kyrgyzstan and Tajikistan, whose economies are comparable with those of the poorer countries of Asia.

These comparisons, however must be used with care. The figures look different when the burden of debt is taken into account. The estimated indebtedness of the countries of Central and Eastern Europe is around 6% of their GNP. For the countries of sub-Saharan Africa and the other highly indebted countries, the figure is around 40%. In many respects comparisons are difficult. In many developing countries the free market has resulted in a stark contrast between the usually powerful, rich upper-class and the poor masses. Although the rise of the black market in Eastern Europe is threatening to create this kind of situation, the contrast between rich and poor is not yet on this kind of scale.

However, it is clear that now is the time to draw upon the expertise of those familiar with the problems of developing countries. They have a head start.
It is for this reason that I am greatly in favour of linking policy in these two areas. Let us not make the same mistakes in the East as were made in the South.

Take, for example, the inferior position of women. In Eastern Europe, as elsewhere, it is the women who work double time. One only has to look at the queues outside the shops. Those rules which favoured women under the old system, such as childcare and the law on abortion, are now threatened. In the new, free market economy, it is more convenient officially not to let women compete in the labour market. Of course things will be different in practice. Just as in the South – and, indeed, here – women will have somehow to scrape together an income from the unofficial economy.

Must they now be forgotten in our policy for the next 20 years? I have heard nothing about women in projects in this area. It is disturbing to see that the proportion of women involved in politics under the old regimes (though I realize that their influence was limited) has fallen from levels as high as 37% to 6%, or even 3%. And what about the environment? Are all the major infrastructure projects which we are now about to launch in the East going to be subjected to an environmental impact assessment? These questions must be linked at EC level, too – perhaps particularly at EC level.

It will also be important to examine the effect of the changes in Eastern Europe in the light of experiences in the South. Even a superficial examination of world trade flows shows that trends towards the normalization of East-West relations may bring great shifts in trade. (At present the volume of trade between the OECD countries and the South is about 15 times as large as between the OECD countries and the East; by comparison the total GNP of the middle and low income countries of the South, taken together, stood at US$ 3 100 billion in 1989 and that of the Central and Eastern European countries at around US$ 1 600 billion[6]. Unsurprisingly, then, calculations show that the normalization of East-West trade may result in a five to ten-fold increase in trade flows as compared with the preceding period[7]. We can only guess at the consequences of this for the developing countries. One thing is, however, clear: development cooperation must abandon its defensive posture and take the initiative.

Openness in government and public finance, a democratic system and respect for human rights are essential preconditions for economic recovery, or rather development. This is a live issue today as the EC, too, is now aware. On 28 November 1991 the Development Council adopted a resolution on human rights, democracy and conditionality. Like the World Bank, the Council made the connection between a country's arms expenditure and expenditure on social items such as education.

This, however, will not on its own be enough. Human rights, as we have understood them hitherto, must more than ever be linked to the question of what is really meant by development. Let us take the example of Guatemala. Recently I returned from a human rights mission there. 60% of the population is descended from the Mayas, an Indian tribe, but this group fill less than 3% of government posts. Poverty among the Indians is severe. Between 85 and 97% of Indian women are illiterate. The Guatemalan Government denies that there is any ethnic problem. For 500 years the Indians have been exploited, driven from their land or slaughtered. One bishop told us that for many years it had been the intention to wipe out the Indians completely. Even now, this process is still going on. How many people in the rest of the world know that 100 000 Indians were murdered between 1979 and 1983?

Tens of thousands of Indians have withdrawn to two places in the north of Guatemala, one high in the mountains, the other deep in the jungle, to escape the army. In these areas, known as CPR (Communities In Resistance) a de facto civil war is being waged. Our delegation split up, and I remained in the mountains for two days. Tens of thousands of Indians have rebuilt their villages there in the past few years in conformity with their traditional way of life.

The Guatemalan Government is currently on peace talks in Mexico with the resistance movement. Inevitably the biggest stumbling block, the central issue, is land. After 10 years in the mountains or the jungle, the Indians wish to stay there and be left alone. Mr Bentfeld, the (white) Minister of Development Cooperation, who is also involved in the peace negotiations, told us that this would only be possible if it could be proved that the land did not belong to anyone else. In that case it would be state land and, in the minister's words, 'the Indians can then buy it from us'.

This I find hard to take. After 500 years, the world is turned upside down. Driven from their best land, to which they have the longest-standing claim, to the last pieces of no-man's land, the Indians are now graciously permitted to buy land which is theirs already. This is the logical consequence of racial segregation. The white descendants of European settlers are continuing to exploit the Indians under the pretext of modernization and development.

All the Indians want is to be left alone, to maintain the forest as a source of life, as it has been for thousands of years, and trouble no one. Where else in the world can one be so hospitably welcomed? What, in these circumstances, is civilization? What is development? What are we to think of the glossy book of photos which the minister proudly showed us of an EC project: model villages to be built on a barren expanse of land for the resettlement of returning refugees from Mexico or displaced forest dwellers: little boxes with corrugated iron roofs in the burning sun? Where have we seen this sort of thing before?

It is true that human rights seem to be becoming an increasingly important factor in the EC's foreign and development policy. That is a step in the right direction, but we must remain vigilant. What are our standards, what criteria are we using? It is not the President of the United States who determines or maintains the world order. Whose order is it, then, and who benefits from it? The EC itself must be consistent and not use double standards. Why have we halted aid to Sudan while trade relations with China are being reopened? What is the logic behind this?

Human rights are a sensitive issue. The events in East Timor in Indonesia, for example, have led to heated debate in the European Parliament, resulting in an almost unanimous resolution strongly condemning Indonesia. Since the adoption in 1991 by the European Council of Development Cooperation Ministers of a resolution on human rights, democracy and conditionality, the sensitive issue of East Timor keeps appearing on the agenda, and still the EC does not know what common position it should take up. For some Member States, trade relations with Indonesia are paramount. The Netherlands, the former colonial power in what used to be the Dutch East Indies, finds this particularly difficult. Between the two government parties, the Social Democrats and the Christian Democrats, there is a wide divergence of views on attitudes to Indonesia. The Christian Democrats are not in favour of strong intervention on human rights in Indonesia. On the other hand, the Social Democrat Minister for Development and Cooperation, Mr Pronk, has reacted fiercely. He seems to have the greater support in Europe, and certainly in the European Parliament.

Like Parliament, the Commission under the aegis of Jacques Delors must also develop its concept of human rights. For what are civilization or development without human rights? Development, democracy and human rights are inextricably bound up together. In my view, the Guatemalan Indians, the forest dwellers of Sarawak and Rwanda, the street children of

Brazil or the women for sale in Thailand should all be put at the top of the agenda. The position of women and children worldwide is still worsening. The traffic in human beings is on the increase. The human body has become an item of goods for sale. Standards and values are declining. Cultures like that of the forest dwellers are threatened with disappearance. It is high time for a new vision of development to be worked out. Let us start with Indians, street children in Guatemala, In India or Brazil, or prostitutes in Bangkok. Western culture should put its arrogance aside. Perhaps then we will finally start to answer the question of what constitutes development.

The EC claims to be a champion of democracy. In its own way, it is joining the chorus of support for Mr Bush's 'New World Order'. To what extent is this a legitimate position? Maastricht has now become the buzz-word in Europe and an immense political row has broken out on the implementation of this 'monster treaty'. Precisely because of the political upheavals and the social and economic problems in Eastern Europe, Western Europe has no choice but to pursue its course of cooperation and integration. The Maastricht Treaty, however, has clearly shown that this process is going too quickly for many EC citizens. In Denmark the Treaty was rejected by an extremely slim majority. In France the opposite happened: an extremely slim majority voted in favour. The fact that such a large proportion of society (49% in France) is against the Treaty represents a serious political risk which demands the politicians undivided attention.

European Union, then, however politically desirable or indeed necessary, arouses a great deal of uncertainty among European citizens. One reason for this is no doubt the fear of losing democratic control. As yet, very few people can fathom the way of Brussels. In the Netherlands, for example, about 40% of legislation is now subject to regulations from Brussels. Mr Delors, the President of the Commission, recently said that when the Maastricht Treaty enters into force, on average 60% of national legislation will be guided by Brussels. The legislative and decision-making processes and the working procedures of the bureaucracy are so opaque that a local or regional action group is in danger of losing its way before it has begun. Increasingly, only a small upper crust will be able to afford the luxury of a costly lobby office in Brussels.

This threatens to create a second democratic deficit which may be more dangerous than the first. The first democratic deficit refers to the fact that, under the Maastricht Treaty, the national parliaments of a number of Member States will lose more powers than the European Parliament gains. In other words there will be a net loss of democracy in the Member States. However, it will be much more dangerous if large sections of society turn against this additional level of government. This situation will create immensely fertile ground for the rise of nationalism: it is a disaster waiting to happen. To see where this can lead us, we only need to look at current events in the former Yugoslavia. When I listen to le Pen in France, I can only shudder.

Europe is therefore faced with a frightful dilemma. Born as I was after the Second World War, my education gave me sufficient historical awareness to realize the necessity of union. One only needs to consider the centuries of conflict in Europe to realize that a few decades of peace are a fragile thing. In fact, we are still faced with the task of building a new world on the debris of the old Europe. Germany and France must not be left alone again by the other Member States. In other words the train of European union must go through, even if it travels so fast that more and more people fall off.

A small group of initiates are forever thinking up new structures, often with immense implications. What are we to think, for example, of my German colleague Klaus Hänsch's proposal, after enlargement of the EC, to do away with the lesser used languages as working languages, to exclude the small countries from the EC's rolling presidency and to abolish the small countries' automatic right to appoint commissioners? I have nothing against Germany's new-found self-confidence, but this should lead to harmony and not to hegemony, which would provide further fuel for the threat of nationalism. Nevertheless, Mr Hänsch's suggestion does address a real problem. How long can the present Community continue to grow before it becomes unworkable? And how real is the proposal by a number of Member States to continue with parts of Maastricht, such as Economic and Monetary Union, with only a few Member States? And what will then be left of the European Union?

What are the hidden dangers of not carrying on a public debate and failing to point out options, advantages and disadvantages? What will happen if discontent begins to arise, rightly or wrongly, at the idea of loss of identity? Will the major parties, and particularly the European Social Democrats, not take the blame for this? That, too, may fan the flames of nationalism. Public debate is absolutely essential, both for ourselves and for the world at large!

However we present it, the democratic content of Europe is of decisive importance for the poorer regions of the world. An undemocratic Europe can never be good news for them. Democracy, human rights and development, the disappearance of old cultures and indigenous peoples, the increasing division between rich and poor, the destruction of the environment and the tropical rain forest, wars, refugees and migration, increased poverty among women, the uprooting of children, bought and sold like property, and our fixation with economic growth, all these things together give the impression of a world society running out of control. These processes, seen in context, are the challenge with which we are faced.

Notes

1. P. Muus, 'Angst EG voor immigratie Sovjet-Unie onterecht' (EC focus of Soviet immigration unjustified), Staatscourant 242, Thursday 12 December 1991.
2. World Development report 1991.
3. World debt tables 1991-1992.
4. Human development report 1991.
5. Source: World Bank.
6. Human development report 1990.
7. Jepma, ESB 18/25-12-91.

9. Migrants, Refugees and Minorities in the New Europe[1]

JAN NIESSEN

Introduction

Although the socio-economic and cultural gap between East and West Europe is still very wide, the end of the political divide between these two parts of Europe offers good opportunities to build a more united and democratic continent. In the wake of the major changes Europe is undergoing, we are, however, witness to the rise of chauvinistic nationalism, racism and xenophobia leading to civil wars in Yugoslavia and the Caucasus, and to violent attacks on refugees, asylum-seekers, immigrants and minorities in many European countries. At the same time, there is the danger that the so-called Third World will drift off the map of Europe's concern. European countries and economic blocs are fiercely protecting their economic interests and are closing their doors to more people who are forced to migrate. In other words, Europe is standing before the challenge of shaping a more united continent that is democratic and open to the world.

In this article we will look at this challenge from the angle of migratory movements within and towards Europe, and the protection of the rights of minorities. How Europe will deal with both questions is crucial for the shaping of the new Europe. Postwar migratory movements (chapter I) have reinforced the traditionally multi-cultural character of most European countries (chapter II). Governments are increasingly working together in areas such as refugees and immigration, social integration and policies to address the root causes of forced migration. The emphasis is more on the control of migratory movements than on the protection of the rights of migrants, refugees and minorities (chapter III). Non-governmental organisations will have to face this situation and renew their efforts to define and uphold the rights of these people (chapter IV).

The reader must be warned that, within the limits set to this article, it will be impossible to do full justice to the varying situations in the various parts of Europe. Moreover, the overall situation in Europe is rapidly changing. In Western Europe the process of further economic and political integration was given a major impetus in the eighties but has seemed to stagnate somewhat in the early nineties. In Eastern Europe the outcome of the disintegration process of the former Soviet Union can hardly be predicted. It seems to be justified to refer to Western and Eastern Europe as in former days, although this is no longer in a geo-political sense (the capitalist West versus the communist East), but in a socio-economic sense (the social market in the West and the developing democracies in the East).

I Migratory movements within and towards Europe

Most, if not all, countries in the world are affected by movements of people, be it as receiving or as sending countries or as both. People are moving for various reasons: to flee from wars, poverty, repression and persecution or, on a voluntary basis, to find work and build a new life elsewhere. As far as Europe is concerned, throughout its history political and socio-economic developments have brought about migratory movements within the old continent but, equally, millions of migrants and refugees from elswhere have settled and become citizens in European countries.

Post war migration has been beneficial for many European

countries and has led to obligations towards the migrant communities (and their countries of origins). In the near future, certain European countries will, again, be in need of migrants. At the same time, the present political and socio-economic situation in the world, including Europe, is leading to an increasing number of refugees, asylum seekers and migrants, making it even more necessary that Europe fulfills international human rights obligations.

1. Migration for employment

Western Europe

After the Second World War countries in North-Western Europe recruited foreign workers on a temporary basis to build up their economies which were ravaged by the war. At first recruiting countries such as Great Britain, France and the Netherlands turned to former colonies. Other countries turned to Italy, Greece and Turkey. Sweden turned to Finland. At a later stage migrant workers were recruited from countries on the southern rim of the Mediterranean basin. Since the socio-economic situation in the countries of origin did not improve and since they were needed for longer than expected in the host countries, temporary migrants had to prolong their stay time and again. By now, one can safely assume that the majority have established themselves permanently.

From the early eighties onwards the traditional sending countries in Southern Europe turned into receiving countries themselves, attracting people mostly from the so-called Third World. Finland recruited workers from the Baltic states.

Today there are between 15 and 20 million immigrants in west, north and south Europe, that is between 4 and 6% of the total population. Among them are many Europeans. For example, out of the about 13 million immigrants living in the

European Community, 5 million coming from other EC member states and 8 million from third-countries, including Scandinavian countries, Switzerland, Austria and Yugoslavia.
Settled migrants and refugees form the so-called groups of 'new or ethnic minorities'. These groups must be distinguished from various kinds of 'traditional minorities' in these parts of Europe, like, for example, the Roma, Sinti and Sami, 'religious minorities', like protestants in Southern Europe and 'national minorities', like the Basques, Catalans and Bretons.

In the mid seventies official recruitment came to a halt in most countries. Nevertheless, there is still an increase in the number of foreigners for reasons like natural increase and family reunification. At the same time, there is a considerable and still increasing number of so-called undocumented or illegal migrants (there are estimates of two million persons) in almost every Western European country. They play a vital role in certain sectors of the economy fulfilling low paid and unskilled jobs.
The demand for specific and skilled workers and the need to balance the effects of the grey-ing of the European population, will set small-scale and organized migratory movements in motion. For example, Germany is recruiting low skilled workers from Poland on a temporary basis. Portugal is in need of construction workers and is turning towards its former African colonies to recruit them.

Eastern Europe
Within the former Soviet-Union various migratory movements took place from one Soviet Republic to another. For example, at present 33% of the Armenians, 21% of the Byelorussians, 18% of the Russians and 15% of the Ukranians live outside their respective countries. Russians account for

38% of the population in Kazakhstan, 34% in Latvia, 30% in Estonia and 22% in the Ukraine. This movement was not so much a 'guest-workers' movement', but more a 'settlers' movement' and it was often based on population policies.
In the former communist countries, the guest-worker system was considered as being a capitalistic phenomenon and it was maintained that this system was non-existent in communist societies. However, large numbers of workers from socialist Third-World countries were recruited on a temporary basis as well. At the end of their contract they are supposed, and often forced, to return to their country of origin. This was, for example, the case with Vietnamese and Mozambicans in the former German Democratic Republic and Czecho-Slovakia. A few of them requested political asylum in Western European countries, but their requests were refused. Movements of temporary workers also took place between Central Europe (Czechoslovakia, the former German Democratic Republic) and Eastern Europe (Russia, Byelorussia).
Over the years, migratory movements from Eastern European countries towards Western Europe were quite effectively curtailed by the former communist regimes, with the exception of relatively small flows of refugees and of skilled workers from Poland and Yugoslavia. It is estimated that between 1948 and 1990 one million Soviet citizens left the Soviet Union of which 40% left after 1985.
The opening up of Eastern Europe has led to new migratory movements within Europe. This is the case between Western and Eastern Europe and between the various Soviet successor states, but also, although to a lesser extent, between Eastern and Central Europe and Eastern/Central Europe and Southern Europe. Among the more than million migrants there are many skilled persons (brain-drain). In the case of the former German Democratic Republic and Albania the fall of the old regimes was preceded by large numbers of people leaving their country ('voting with feet'). Of all Western Eu-

ropean countries Germany receives in the largest number of asylum-seekers and refugees.
European countries are not the only destination but there are others as well, such as the United States, Canada, Israel, Southern Africa and Australia.

2. Refugees and asylum-seekers

World War II and its aftermath have uprooted tens of millions of people. Millions of displaced persons from Eastern Europe have established themselves in Germany and North and South Ameria. Since the early fifties millions of refugees from Europe and elsewhere have been integrated into Western European countries.
Whereas until the mid-seventies about 70% of the total immigration into Western Europe was granted on economic grounds, about 80% of the legal migration is nowadays of non-economic character. Hundreds of thousands of people are admitted on social and humanitarian grounds (family reunification and political asylum).
Of the estimated 15 to 17 million refugees in the world only about 5% are estimated to have settled in Western European countries (1989). This represents 0.5% of the population of these countries. An unknown number of refugees have settled in Eastern European countries, many of them coming from Latin America. Over the last five to ten years the total number of asylum- seekers coming to Western Europe has increased considerably. This poses a growing problem in terms of meeting their needs. The increase has resulted in sizeable backlogs of undecided asylum claims, giving rise to a serious strain on reception facilities and growing expenses for public relief and assistance. It also keeps the persons involved in an uncertain position for a considerable time.
Refugees and asylum-seekers coming to Europe are from Central and Eastern Europe and from Third-World countries

(mainly from Africa, Asia and the Middle East). According to the UNHCR there were 526.130 persons who asked for asylum in Western European States in 1991. The recognition rate in most countries in 1991 is below 15%. For example, Finland has a recognition rate of 1%, Ireland and Greece 2% , Germany 7%, Sweden 8%, Great Britain 11%, Austria 12% and France 13%. The greatest number of asylum-seekers go to Germany (256.112), followed way behind by France (46.784) and Great Britain (44.745). The two latter countries are about the same level as smaller countries such as Switzerland (41.629), Austria (27.306) and Sweden (26.489). In terms of the size of the population Switzerland (1 asylum-seeker in 163 inhabitants), Austria (1 in 278), Germany (1 in 308) and Sweden (1 in 320) receive more asylum-seekers than the other Western European countries (France 1 in 1.197; Great Britain 1 in 1.274 and Ireland, the absolute minimum of 1 in 72.000).
The escalation of the war in ex-Yugoslavia has dramatically increased the numbers of refugees fleeing mainly to Germany, Sweden and Switzerland. For example, it is expected that by the end of 1992 half a million asylum-seekers will have entered Germany.

In Western Europe, but also in the United States and Australia, there is much ado about the definition of a refugee. It is estimated that 80% of the asylum-seekers cannot claim refugee status under the UN Convention on Refugees. Governments have given the name 'economic refugees' to these asylum-seekers. Perhaps this is juridically speaking not correct, but it gives a clear indication as to why people are forced to move, namely the global disparities between rich and poor.
Due to the fact that Europe lacks a well defined immigration policy, a great number of persons are applying for asylum as the only possible way to enter a country legally. They would

have been recruited and employed in times when the demand for labour exceeded the supply. Often those whose request for asylum has been rejected remain in the country where they applied for it and join the so-called clandestine labour force.
A distinction is made between various categories of refugees and asylum-seekers for which the international community will have to assume its responsibility in terms of protection and assistance. Four major categories can be distinguished:

a. Those who apply for the status of refugee on the basis of a well-founded fear of being persecuted for reasons of race, religion, nationality and membership of a particular group or political opinion (definition according to the United Nations Convention relating to the Status of Refugees).

b. Those who flee because of wars, social upheavals, external aggression, foreign domination and occupation (definition according to the Organization of African Unity Convention governing the specific aspects of refugee problems in Africa).

c. Those who apply for asylum or seek protection but who do not fall into the terms of these two Conventions or other international agreements and who flee from extreme poverty or because of ecological and natural disasters.

d. Those who flee from violence, wars, extreme poverty, etc. without leaving the country (displaced persons).

Over the last ten years there has been a shift in the type of refugees coming to Europe from the first category to the second and the third. There is a considerable increase in numbers of displaced persons within the former Soviet Union.

3. Future migratory movements

There are an estimated 100 million migrants and refugees in the world. It is very likely, for reasons set out below, that their numbers will grow in the years to come.

Movements towards Europe

Whereas the population of Europe is ageing, 80% of the population of the less developed countries is under 30 years. The population of the developed countries has dropped from one-third of the world's population to one-quarter in twenty five years and will further fall to one-fifth in the year 2000. Europe's prospects for the year 2000 are that its population will amount to 3% of the world's population as against 6% now and in nine countries more than 15% of the population will be over 65 as against two countries now.

At present, life expectancy in the developed countries is 73.1 years and the average fertility rate is a little under two. There is a reversed trend in the developing countries in the world. Within 30 years the population of Sub-Saharan Africa will have grown to one or two billion, of the Maghreb to 150 million, of Egypt to 90 million and of Turkey to 90 million. At present life expectancy of the less developed countries is 57.3 years and the fertility rate stands at about four.

These trends will lead to increasing migration pressures. Whether this will lead to mass migration depends on a number of factors such as, for example, the life expectancy and job opportunities in the less developed countries and the degree of regional and global disparities.

In some 130 of the about 170 States in the world human rights are violated. There are about 70 armed conflicts in the world and it is estimated that 90% of the victims are civilians. In the Cold War era these conflicts were fuelled with the antagonistic positions the super powers took. Divisions

along other lines may occur easily (the rich against the poor; the Western world against the Islamic world).
If things do not change rapidly, 600 million people will be suffering from malnutrition by the year 2000. Ecological changes are rapidly taking place. Each year the Sahara increases in an area equal to the size of a country like Hungary and further cutting down the rain forest will have disastrous consequences.
All these developments will dramatically decrease the life expectancy of millions of people and many of them will have to migrate or flee in order to survive.
An estimated 60 million young persons enter the labour market of the least developed countries each year for which 30 to 40 million new jobs have to be created. Given the overall economic situation of these countries this seems highly unlikely. It is a well known fact that there is a reverse relationship between the capacity of incorporating workers into the labour force and migratory movements.
Looking at the present situation it becomes clear that the disparities between rich and poor countries persist and that the current policies of the richest countries in the world are widening rather than closing the gap. Consequently the number of people forced to build up a life elswhere will increase. Although this is very much feared by European governments and large sectors of the European populations, it is highly unlikely that all those who are forced to migrate will head for Europe. The majority will stay temporarily or settle in countries near their countries of origin. The newly industrialised countries, particularly in Asia, will also attract large numbers of migrants.

Movements within Europe

It is not realistic to expect that the migratory movements, triggered off by, or immediately preceding, the political changes in Eastern Europe, will come to an end in the years

to come. It is very hard to say how many people will actually migrate. Clearly, political leaders of Eastern European countries have grossly exaggerated the numbers of people that would migrate. They may have done so to convince the world that, in order to prevent this, huge economic investments were needed. Western European countries, on the contrary, have used these inflated figures to tighten their admission policies.
The following categories of migrants and refugees can be distinguished.

a. Migration based on ethnic affinity. More than one million people left the former Soviet Union all of whom can claim that their ancestors were German, Greek, Korean, etc. For centuries they kept their own identity, culture and religion. This is the case with Jews, ethnic Germans, Poles, Greeks, Finns and Koreans.

b. Return migration. Starting already in the early eighties, many Russians who have settled themselves in Soviet Republics returned to Russia from Central Asian and Caucasian Soviet successor states. It is expected that more Russians will follow in the years to come (this year alone 500.000 are expected). Other former Soviet people may decide to return as well such as, for example, the Tartars living in the Crimea.
   African and Asian temporary migrant workers in Central Europe will (have to) return to their country of origin.

c. Forced migration as a result of ethnic conflicts. This is the case of, for example: the Roma (gypsy) people from Romania and ex-Yugoslavia to notably Germany, Hungary and Poland; Turks from Bulgaria (and back again); Hungarians from Romania.

d. Refugee movements. Separatism and chauvinistic nationalism has led to wars in the Balkans and the Caucasus resulting in refugee flows to Western, Central and Southern Europe and to Soviet successor states.
   It must not be ruled out that in the near future authoritarian regimes will be established in Central Asian republics or elsewhere in the former Soviet Union. This will certainly lead to new flows of refugees.

e. Migration for economic reasons. The restructuring of the economies of the former communist countries, from centrally directed to market economies, will lead to many frictions in society (unemployment, stagnation of the provision of services and goods). At present there are hundreds of thousands of people trying to find a temporary or permanent job in a country other than the one in which they live, for example Ukrainians and Russians move to Central Europe (business tourism and itinerant workers), Poles to Germany (contract workers), etc.

f. Displaced persons. On the territory of the Russian Federation there are about 250.000 displaced persons who are concentrated in and around Moscow, Rostov, Stavropol and St. Petersburg. They come from Azerbaijan, South Ossetia, Georgia, Turkmenistan, Tajikistan and Uzbekistan.

II Culturally and racially diverse Europe[2]

Europe has always been a continent from which people migrated to almost every other continent. Partly this is the history of European colonization and domination of large parts of the world. Partly it is the history of the poor and oppressed people of Europe who, in the struggle to survive, had to leave the continent.

There have always been large migratory movements towards and within the old continent as well. The post-war migratory movements towards North Western Europe add a new chapter to the history of migration. However, many European societies have difficulties in coming to terms with the new situation. In Eastern Europe a period has come to an end where national and ethnic identities were suppressed by a centralistic power in the name of the unity of the workers' state.

Multi-cultural Europe

European countries have always been multicultural societies and have been open to influences from other cultures. The presence of new groups of ethnic minorities has added to this diversity in a distinctive way. Firstly, because of the relative rapidity with which groups with varying cultures entered and subsequently settled into European countries. Secondly, because of the relatively small size of the groups which are often concentrated in urban areas and which have striking cultural differences with 'the' culture of the receiving societies.

The full participation of new minorities demands the cultural adjustment of both the ethnic groups and the society as a whole. The new minorities are challenged to accommodate and to participate in a new way of life while maintaining their own identity. On the other hand, the host community must be prepared to appreciate cultural differences and to create a climate of openness. There is a relationship between, on the one hand, the distance between the culture of the minority groups and of the receiving society and, on the other, the ease with which minorities can fully participate in the host societies.

It is not easy to try and summarize the differences between 'the European culture' and 'the culture of ethnic minorities', but they could broadly be described as follows. Migrants and

refugees are living in a secularized christian society with a strong materialistic and individualistic culture, whereas in the societies they come from culture, religion and community-life still play a vital, if not dominant, role.
It goes without saying that this harbours enough elements for conflict. The new minorities will find it difficult to maintain and adapt their values without losing their very heart. Europeans find it difficult to accept that their basic values are not taken at face value, are challenged or even rejected. The present debate focusses very much on the differences between Western and Islamic values.

Multi-religious Europe
Europe has traditionally been considered to be a Christian continent with Roman Catholic, Greek and Russian Orthodox and Reformed traditions. The East, with the dominance of Orthodox churches, was more monolithic and the West, partly Roman Catholic and partly Protestant, was more pluralistic. In some European countries there are Muslim minorities (for example, ex-Yugoslavia), or remnants of a Muslim culture (for example, in Spain and Portugal). Turkey, the bridge between Asia and Europe, is a Muslim country. The majority of the religious Albanians are Muslims and, of course, in some (Asian) Soviet successor states the whole or the majority of the population is Muslim.
A long process of secularization and separation of church and state mean that Europe as a whole can no longer consider itself a Christian continent. To define its cultural and religious identity, references are made in Western Europe to the Judeo-Christian and Humanistic heritage. The situation in Eastern Europe is different to that in Western Europe. For three quarters of this century the official ideology was atheist and religious freedom was suppressed. In Central Europe the Catholic and Protestant churches played an important role in bringing about the fundamental changes. They have been an

effective vehicle for protest and now they are trying to build up their churches again.

Nowadays, millions of Muslims, Hindus and Sikhs are living in Western Europe. In some European countries Muslims outnumber Protestants or Roman Catholics.

The debates on multi-culturalism centre around values which quite often refer to religion or to 'sacred' humanistic values. This is due not only to two recent affairs involving the Muslim communities in various European countries (the Rushdie-affair and the scarves-affair), but also to the age-old and complicated relationship between the Arab/Muslim and the European/Christian civilization. The two have been at war regularly from 732 onwards and are competitors in the realms of religion, science and art. From the time Arab and Muslim countries were colonized until today, all Muslim and Arab resistance against Western political, economic and cultural dominance has been considered to be based on religious fundamentalism. For their part Muslims stereotype Western cultural values as pernicious and they condemn the permissiveness of Western societies.

Not only is the distance between Muslim and European cultural traditions considered to be large, but this is also the case of other minority groups and Europeans (for example, Hindus, Sikhs and African religious traditions).

The new minorities find themselves in a similar position to many of their countries of origin. Both are being culturally, socially and politically marginalized, the new minorities within European societies and the countries of origin in a world that is dominated by Europe, the United States and Japan. In this context the culture and religious beliefs of the minorities are seen to be a refuge against Western dominance. They are also weapons against Western feelings of superiority and racism with which both the countries of origin and the minorities are confronted. Further marginalization could turn this orientation into fundamentalism and radicalism.

On the other side, Europeans are stressing their cultural identity expressing fears that the presence of, in their view, so many culturally different groups endangers the cohesiveness of society. One step further and one's 'national' identity will be considered superior to other cultures. In the Roman Catholic church there are powerful groups that openly plea for a re-christianisation of the whole of Europe. Fundamentalistic Protestants have a similar agenda. In the Ukraine the Orthodox church has become a player in the nationalistic movement.
Undoubtedly, this will all have a negative effect on relations between the culturally and religiously diverse communities in Europe.

Diversity
Migrants and refugees come from all over the world. They have different cultural and political backgrounds. Even people coming from the same country may not share a common cultural heritage. In some countries or big cities one can find over hundred nationalities. This makes it difficult for migrants, refugees and the local population to build a cohesive community. Furthermore, social policies have to cope with this diversity of the sometimes mutually exclusive cultures and different political backgrounds of all the minority groups.
Among the largest groups in Western Europe are persons from the Maghreb (France, Spain, the Netherlands), Turkey (Germany, Sweden) and the Indian sub-continent (United Kingdom). Other relatively large groups are Caribbeans (France, United Kingdom, the Netherlands), Philippinos (Spain, Greece, Italy), Black Africans (France, United Kingdom, Belgium), Yugoslavs (Germany), Polish (France, Germany), Swiss (France), Portuguese (France, Luxembourg, Spain), Spaniards (France), Italians (Germany, Switzerland, France, Belgium), Greeks (Germany, Sweden), Scandinavians (Denmark) etc.

The diversity in Central and Eastern Europe dates back to the end of last century from the fall of the Ottoman, Austro-Hungarian and Russian empires. New nation states were created which included various ethnic minorities or where boundaries cut across areas where the same people were living. This led to ethnic tensions and large-scale migratory and refugee movements, lasting until World War II after which a period of containment started. This period came to an end in the late eighties resulting once more in migratory movements.

Concentration

The idea that Western Europe is flooded with foreigners has no factual basis. It is in fact the concentration of 'foreigners' which gives some people this idea. In almost every Western European country more than half of the new ethnic minorities live in urban and industrial areas. The houses they live in are often very old and run-down, because they have been inhabited intensively by many generations of workers. Usually house owners – both private and public – spend too little on up-keep which has also contributed to their decay. Moreover, the building or renovation of houses has not kept pace with developments in the labour market for which many migrants were recruited in a short time. Because of that many families were forced to share their house with others. In some areas low cost housing estates were quickly built on too few square meters.

This relative over-population leads to strains on public facilities (such as schools, day-care centres, health services, sport and leisure facilities). The local labour market is not able to absorb the growing number of (mostly young) persons seeking a job.

Competition

The ongoing restructuring of the economies and the economic recession have tremendous effects on societies. In

Western Europe the social market economy, resulting in the welfare state, is being put under pressure. There is a high rate of unemployment all over Europe. In the European Community alone there are 40 million poor people and the unemployment rate stands at 10% in 1992. In Eastern Europe the situation is even more worrying, possibly with the exception of a few Central European countries. It is particularly young people who are out of work.
This creates a climate whereby the interests of European nations, and within these nations the interest of nationals, are put first. The invaluable contribution of migrant workers to the building up of the welfare state is easily forgotten, even when studies show that in many countries migrants workers still cannot be missed. Moreover, many migrant workers have become smaller or bigger entrepreneurs contributing substantially to the economics of the host countries.
As said, more than half of the new ethnic minorities live in urban and industrial areas. Since budgets of cities seldom allow extra spending and national governments usually do not provide the necessary extra funding, the different groups often end up in a competition for the scarce means available for social, cultural and educational activities. Problems most frequently arise in urban areas where not only many migrants and refugees live but also indigenous people who often have a weak socio-economic position. Their resistance to foreigners is not necessarily racist but is also an expression of their protest against the fact that they have to share the scarce housing and welfare facilities with even more people.

Discrimination in the labour market
Being employed is of vital importance to immigrants and refugees. It keeps them self-reliant whereas being unemployed makes them reliant on social assistance and undermines their participation in society. In most countries the number of unemployed migrants and refugees is disproportionately

higher than compared with the national population. Among the unemployed, the majority consists of women and youth. Both refugees and migrants are often accused of taking jobs away from nationals, but when unemployed they are accused of taking advantage of the social security system.

Unlike recruited migrant workers, refugees arrive without a job and they are confronted with many difficulties to find one. According to the Geneva Convention recognized refugees should be granted the right to work and be equally treated with other foreigners. Quite often refugees with specialized skills find themselves working at jobs for which they are overqualified.

Most migrant workers are originally recruited as unskilled workers to fill the temporary gap between supply and demand in the labour market. Due to technological changes in the production process unskilled labour has become increasingly but not totally superfluous. This partly explains the high unemployment rate among migrants. They were hardest hit by these changes. Their children are relatively under-represented in secondary education and over-represented in primary education, which explains, again partly, why many of them have not succeeded in finding more qualified jobs. To compensate for the drop in family income many wives have taken up work in cleaning services and as domestics. They also take up low-paid house labour.

However, other factors also play a role. There is a built-in mechanism in the labour market which keeps ethnic minorities in an unfavourable position as to the kind of work and promotion opportunities. Proportionally more immigrants than nationals can be found in low paid and low skilled jobs. However, it is still not easy for immigrants to gain promotion after having reached a certain level of responsibility in a company (the famous glass ceiling). When out of a job, immigrants have more difficulties than nationals to find another one. Employers quite often seem to prefer native workers and the latter in turn are inclined to monopolize the labour market.

Racism and xenophobia

Due to similar and different circumstances in the various parts of Europe racism and xenophobia are on the rise. It is, for example, a well-known fact that social and economic deprivation of large groups of people is a breeding ground for racism and xenophobia. This is clearly the case in the urban and industrial centres in decline in countries as France, Great Britain, Germany, Belgium and the Netherlands, but also in the former German Democratic Republic and Czechoslovakia. In these strongholds of labour, socialist and communist parties, right wing political parties and movements have gained considerable ground during the last ten years.

More sophisticated forms of racism can be found in theories of superiority of Western culture, values and political system. These views are held by many persons belonging to the middle and upper classes.

Over the last twenty years there have been outbreaks of racial attacks against black people, ethnic and national minorities (among them the Sinti and Roma peoples) and refugees in many parts of Europe, from Sweden to Italy, from the Netherlands to Switzerland, from Great Britain to Russia. Almost everywhere in Europe there is a revival of anti-semitism and anti-arabism. In France and Germany graves of Jews are desecrated. Arabs in France and Spain are frequently harassed and killed. The recent attacks on Roma, refugees, immigrants and blacks all over Germany (1800 attacks this year alone resulting in the killing of 16 persons, among them children) give reason to believe that these attacks are fairly well orchestrated.

There is evidence that extremist groups are working together in Europe. Among them are groups of neo-nazis, skin-heads

and football hooligans. Right wing political parties, such as the British National Front, the German Republikaner, the Belgian Vlaams Blok and the French Front National, have their international networks and some of these parties are even represented in the European Parliament.
Political parties on the extreme right are gaining ground and, what is even more dangerous, some of their ideas are being taken over by mainstream political parties. This is for example the case with liberal parties (liberal in Europe often means conservative) in Austria and Belgium. But also Christian- Democratic (in most cases centre right parties) and Social-Democratic parties are under pressure to give in to populist racialist and xenophobic demands.

Racial hatred and violent attacks on immigrants, blacks and everyone who looks like a 'foreigner' has led to fear among these communities. Sooner or later the violence against them will incite some of them to strike back in a similar way.

Chauvinistic nationalism
Whereas in Western Europe there is a process of further social and political co-operation and unification, in Eastern Europe the opposite takes place. In all parts of Europe these opposite trends entail similar possibilities for national and ethnic minorities to express themselves. However, everywhere in Europe the danger of chauvinistic nationalism looms large and this could lead, and in some cases has already led, to wars and the dis-integration of (parts of) societies.
The rise of nationalism in Western Europe can be explained by a number of factors. One is the failure of the political system or ruling political parties to solve the problems of the country. In this case nationalistic movements plea for the dissolution of a state (Italy) or the transformation of it into a federation (Belgium). These movements or certain sectors of

them started blaming not only the 'central government' but also the 'foreigner'. In Scotland the nationalistic movement has a democratic character and strives for a greater autonomy within the United Kingdom. Nationalism is also a reaction against what is seen to be a loss of national identity because of the process of further unification in the framework of the of the European Communities. Although this is not necessarily racist, the debates, for example, in France and England on the so-called Maastricht Treaty had clear xenophobic undertones.

In Central and Eastern Europe nationalistic movements are to a great extent a reaction against the dominance of Moscow as the guardian of the unity of the workers' state. In this ideology and, of course, for geo-political reasons, national identity was seen as a threat. The nationalistic movements in a number of Soviet Union Republics have set in motion the process leading to independence (in the Baltics, for example).

However, every nationalistic movement runs the risk that the plea for greater national autonomy or the call for a strong national identity will turn into chauvinistic nationalism.

Civil and political rights

Western European countries have become countries of immigration. The guest workers have turned into settlers. Immigration still takes place on humanitarian grounds and on the basis of selective recruitment. The problem is that most European countries do not acknowledge this fact. The absence of a clear immigration policy opens the door for arbitrary judgements as to who will be admitted for which purpose.

Another effect is that there is a clear lack of a policy gradually granting all civil and political rights (including voting rights) to those who are legally resident in a European

country without being of the nationality of that country. Millions of 'guestworkers' who have been resident for over 5 or 10 years in Western European countries are still being considered foreigners, their social and legal position being far from secure.
Naturalization is a possible but not an easy route to be followed by the de facto immigrants because of the often lengthy and costly procedures. In the global village of today, where improved means of communication make people not only more mobile but also easier at home at more than one place, the concept of dual nationality is still not widely accepted. Many Member States of the Council of Europe have ratified a Convention that forbids dual citizenship.

In the former Soviet Union the situation has arisen turning what once was internal migration within the Union into international migration between Soviet successor states. This has a great impact on the question of citizenship. Soviet citizenship ceased to exist raising questions as to the status of former Soviet citizens living in a successor state other than their own. This is a very pressing issue in the Baltic Republics of Estonia and Latvia where a large numbers of Russians live.

III European policies

The end of the political divide between East and West Europe offers good opportunities to build a more united and democratic continent that should live up to international human rights obligations, including those of migrant workers, refugees and minorities. There are a good many fora and political institutions at work in Europe and political leaders and high ranking civil servants meet regularly to discuss common interests and concerns. Migration and the protection of minorities rank high on the agenda. In Western Europe alone more than 100 meetings on this subject took place in 1991 and within the European Community there are about 30 working groups. Governments in Europe are increasingly working together in areas as refugees and immigration, social integration of minorities and policies to address root causes of migration.

1. International bodies

The Conference of Security and Co-operation in Europe (CSCE)
The CSCE, also known as the Helsinki process, started in 1973 and has resulted in quite a number of (pan) European Charters and Acts promoting the co-operation between Western Europe (and the United States and Canada) and Eastern Europe in areas such as security and peace, economic co-operation and human rights. The CSCE played a very important role during the cold war era when it functioned as a platform for information and dialogue. At present 52 states are members and the CSCE is changing its character from a 'process' to a more institutionalized organization. Offices have been set up in Prague and Warsaw which must implement the decisions taken within the framework of the CSCE. In November 1992 a seminar on tolerance was organized by the Prague office and in April 1993 the Warsaw office will organize a seminar on migratory movements.
The free movement of persons has always ranked high on the agenda of the CSCE, as well the protection of human rights of citizens and, recently, of minorities. The CSCE was less outspoken about refugees (back on the CSCE agenda largely due to pressures from NGOs) and migrant workers. The concluded CSCE Agreements or Acts are juridically speaking not binding and enforcable. Politically and morally they carry considerable weight. NGOs can refer to them in their activities to defend the rights of migrants, refugees and minorities.

The CSCE offers good opportunities for NGOs to monitor human rights policies in Europe and to present their concerns to the governments of the states involved.

The Council of Europe

The Council of Europe (with its headquarters in Strasbourg, France) was founded in 1949 by Western European states and has at present 27 Member States. Since the opening up of Eastern Europe four Eastern European countries have become full members (soon to be followed by the three Baltic Republics), whereas other Eastern European states enjoy the status of observer.

The Council's activities are directed towards the promotion of civil, political, cultural and social rights. The Council has a longstanding tradition of concern with the situation of migrants in Europe. The Council has adopted numerous Conventions, which are binding for the ratifying states, and Resolutions, which are not binding. The Council developed a series of general human rights instruments which are also applicable to the situation of immigrants, refugees and minorities, and special human rights instruments focussing on the position of these groups.

The European Convention on the Protection of Human Rights and Fundamental Freedoms (1950) has, for example, an anti-discrimination provision and it guarantees the right to family reunification. All Member States have ratified the Convention and almost every State has recognized the right to individual complaint. The supervisory mechanism of the Convention is strong. There is the European Human Rights Commission and the European Court of Human Rights which see to the proper implementation of the Convention. They are invaluable instruments in the hands of NGOs. The European Social Charter (1950) is the counterpart of the Human Rights Convention in the field of economic and social rights. Not every Member State has ratified this Convention

and its supervisory mechanism is weak. The European Convention on the Legal Status of Migrant Workers (1977) has only been signed by seven Member States. The Convention promotes equality of treatment of migrant and national workers in the field of recruitment, residence and work permits, family reunion, working conditions, housing, social security, schooling and vocational training, etc.
In the early nineties the Council has organized a series of Ministerial Conferences, such as the Vienna Conference on East-West migration and the Rome Conference on North-South migration.
Several years ago a project was launched named the 'Community relations project', which is now being continued as 'The integration of immigrants: towards equal opportunities'. It brings together governmental experts and NGOs to exchange experiences and to suggest new measures and policies.

NGOs may acquire the status of official observer to the Council of Europe and some have acquired the right to participate in working groups and committees.

The European Community
The policies of the European Communnity (EC) come about through either Community legislation or intergovernmental co-operation between the twelve Member States. This can be explained by the dual character of the Community. Whereas the Council of Europe is an example of international co-operation, the European Community is a mixture of international and supranational co-operation. Community legislation can only be initiated by the European Commission and is endorsed by the Council of Ministers after co-operation or consultation with the European Parliament. It is binding for all Member States and is subject to judicial control by the Court of Justice of the European Communities (Luxembourg).

The European Community's migration policy is limited in scope, namely related to the movement of workers. The Community's activities are directed towards economic integration and, strictly speaking, only towards other areas insofar as they serve that purpose.
Although the EC Treaty laid down principles for Community action favouring the harmonization and approximation of social policies of Member States, it already became clear in the early sixties that many Member States wanted to restrict the legislative powers of the European Commission in this field. This certainly applies to Community action in the field of migration from third-countries (i.e migrants from countries other than EC Member States). The governments want to maintain, as much as possible, their national sovereignty. Nevertheless, the Community has developed a series of binding measures which protect the rights of migrants and their families.
In the seventies the Council of Ministers stressed on more than one occasion the necessity for concerted action aiming at equality of treatment for Community and non-Community workers in respect of living and working conditions, wages and economic rights. Besides, the Member States expressed their intention to promote consultations on immigration policies vis-a-vis third-countries. The question is how this could be organized: either by direct consultations between all Member States (the so-called intergovernmental approach) or by a process within the framework of the Community institutions (the Community approach).
In the eighties, when the question of immigration from third-countries became a burning political issue, the Member States clearly opted for the first choice. A number of intergovernmental working groups were set up, consisting of representatives of either all Member States (such as the notorious Trevi-groups, the Ad Hoc Group on Immigration and the Group of Co-ordinators) or some Member States (such as the

Schengen-group) which prepared, behind closed doors, conventions on refugees or conventions containing paragraphs on immigration and refugees. These groups are also preparing for all kinds of application measures.
In the early nineties migration related issues were among the items on the agenda of the meetings preparing for the famous Maastricht Summit (1991) leading to the adoption of the Treaty on European Union. By this Treaty the intergovernmental approach will be reinforced. An extension of the Community's competence in matters of legal and social integration of immigrants is highly unlikely.

NGOs do not have an officially recognized status of observer to the Community institutions. An increasing number of national NGOs have rightly come to the conclusion that their national lobbying work should be complemented by lobbying in Brussels. In other words the human rights lobby is growing in Brussels (the seat of the European Commission and partly of the European Parliament) and in Strasbourg (the main seat of the Parliament)

The European Community and its neighbours

In 1991 three Association Agreements were signed between the European Community and Hungary, Czechoslovakia and Poland respectively. They contain provisions relating to the movement of workers, services and capital. In the same year an accord was reached between the European Community and the EFTA States on the creation of the European Economic Area. As soon as this Agreement takes effect (probably in January 1993), there will be an area of nineteen European countries where there will be free movement of persons, services and capital. The countries included are the twelve Member States of the European Community and the six EFTA countries Austria, Finland, Iceland, Norway, Sweden and Switzerland (and Liechtenstein being an observer to EFTA).

The conclusion must be that the EC is intensifying its co-operation in matters related to migration and refugees with other European States. This would mean that for the years to come migration policies in Europe will, to a great extent, be determined by the European Community and its Member States.

Over the years many association and co-operation agreements have been concluded between the European Community and other European and non-European countries (for example, with Turkey and the Maghreb countries). In many cases these agreements contain provisions relating to the movement of workers and the protection of their rights. The Community has also concluded the so-called Lomé Convention with African Caribbean and Pacific countries which includes provisions about workers and students. The Annex of Lomé IV contains intentions as regards migrant workers such as the need for respect of the fundamental freedoms, improvement of social and cultural facilities and training projects.

2. Policy developments

Harmonization

Most governments in Western Europe have come to the conclusion that national policies to regulate international migration are doomed to fail. On the other hand, they are very keen to maintain their sovereignty in matters related to immigration. Moreover, they have to take into consideration that the variety of post war immigration has led to a diversity of obligations towards migrant communities and their countries of origin.

The efforts which are being made to harmonize their policies have to reconcile international human rights obligations and the interests of the European states. During the seventies,

the need was felt to develop and implement (inter-) national standards to protect the rights of migrants and refugees. In the eighties, however, policy orientations gradually shifted from this approach to one in which the protection of states' interests predominates and in some cases connects migration with national security. The emphasis is very much on visa and admission policies, the control of migratory movements and the fight against clandestine migration.
The need to harmonize is even more pressing in the case of the European Communities, because as from January 1993 controls at the internal borders between the Member States will be lifted. An area of free travel and movement will come into being. In other words, the admission policy of one Member State immediately has an effect on the others.

Technocracy
There seems to be a great fear that Europe will be flooded with refugees and clandestine migrants. This is reflected in the way European countries conduct their policies on the international level. Within the framework of the Council of Europe various working groups have been set up as a follow-up of the Vienna Conference of 1991. Within the European Community there are many working groups as well (see above). Measures are being prepared behind closed doors without proper consultation with (inter)national parliamentary assemblies and NGOs.
This is, of course, going against the idea of an open and democratic society where parliaments must be fully involved in the decison making processes and where NGOs play their widely recognized and useful role. On the one hand European citizens are called to become European citizens and think European, but, on the other hand, they are confronted with secretive groups preparing measures that will affect not only the lives of ethnic minorities, immigrants and refugees but also their own lives. For example, the abolition of inter-

nal border controls will lead to increased numbers and severity of controls at external borders and at specific places within the countries concerned. This will affect citizens in general and ethnic minorities in particular.

Refugee and asylum policy

Confronted with growing numbers of refugees and asylum-seekers European countries are designing more restrictive policies: ranging from a strict application of the UN Refugee Convention, to measures such as the introduction of a list of safe countries from which no refugees will be accepted, mass deportation, the expulsion of asylum-seekers to the country they first entered after fleeing and which is considered to be safe, visa obligations for refugees, sanctions for air companies transporting persons without valid papers, etc.

The Member States are about to adopt or implement conventions such as the Dublin Convention (which is open for ratification by non-Member States as well) and the 'External Border Crossing Convention'. International working grups of civil servants are preparing all kinds of measures to implement these conventions without being properly controlled by the European and national Parliaments.

Participation policy

It is maintained by some governments that, as long as the international flux of migrants to Europe is not brought under control, policies aiming at integration of legally residing immigrants are bound to fail. This kind of reasoning focusses on the relatively small number of people coming to Europe which is apparently considered to overstretch Europe's reception capacity. It overlooks the fact that there are between 15 to 20 million immigrants who have been living in Europe for quite some time already which, in itself, justifies adequate policies aiming at their full participation in European societies.

Addressing root causes of forced migration

Migratory movements will never be brought under control as long as socio-economic imbalances in the world continue to exist. Fortunately, the idea is gaining ground that root causes of forced migration have to be confronted.

However, there may be a contradiction in European policies. Europe's economic expansion could very well be in conflict with the badly needed policy ensuring investment and aid for developing countries leading to job development and popular participation in economic activity. Moreover, promoting democracy and human rights may be in conflict with economic or geo-political interests.

Most measures to prevent the forced movements of people will have an effect in the medium and long term. They should be implemented alongside and not instead of policies to receive people in Europe on humanitarian grounds and of other forms of protection and assistance of refugees and displaced persons near their regions of origin.

IV The advocacy agenda of NGO's

The international movements of men, women and children require universal standards and instruments to protect their rights. There is a whole number of valuable universal and regional conventions and agreements defining these rights. These conventions are signed and ratified by a great but not sufficient number of States. Nowadays, governments are harmonizing their migration and refugee policies. Whereas – as stated above – during the seventies, the need was felt to develop and implement (inter-) national standards to protect the rights of migrants and refugees, in the eighties, policy orientations gradually shifted from this approach to one of controlling migration flows. Moreover, democracy is at stake when groups of people or minorities are being politically and socially marginalized.

Political parties, trade unions, employers' organizations, churches and other organizations have to assume their responsibility and work together as much as possible in order to avoid a class of second class citizens being created. Europe cannot afford to waste the talents of large numbers of people, but must take advantage of the presence of people with a different cultural background.

There is a clear need for advocacy at the national and international level. The following opportunities for concrete action will focus on a few issues and on the international instruments to work on these issues.

Harmonization
NGOs must press for the signing, ratification and full implementation of the relevant international conventions of the United Nations, the International Labour Organisation and the Council of Europe. The relevant Conventions define the rights and obligations of migrants and refugees, protect against racial discrimination and promote the equality of treatment. This would bring about the desired harmonization.

Protection and assistance
NGOs can press for a policy that promotes respect for human rights worldwide, and for a liberal refugee policy. The Convention (1951) and Protocol (1967) relating to the Status of Refugees must be implemented to the full. European states may be urged to consider adhering to the Convention relating to refugees of the Organization of African Unity which recognizes wars and social upheavals as a valid ground for application for asylum.
Conventions concluded between all or some Member States of the European Community, such as the Dublin Convention and the Schengen Treaty, must be amended in such a way

that the existing European Courts are declared competent to rule on matters related to the implementation of such Conventions. NGOs must plea for democratic control of the implementation measures which are being prepared by international working groups which meet behind closed doors.
NGOs should also reflect on how protection and assistance can be given to refugees and displaced persons near the place from where they are fleeing. The efforts of the newly created UN Under-Secretariat for Humanitarian Affairs need a critical but co-operative response from NGOs.

Combating racism
A wide range of programmes is needed, from education to change people's attitudes, to affirmative action to bring about equality of treatment for all.
Whatever programme is adopted and carried out, the banning of all forms of discrimination, xenophobia and racism must have a firm basis in national and international law. National legislation must outlaw discriminatory and racial behaviour, and promote equality of treatment. The ratification and full implementation of existing international instruments can support and complement national legislation and, in case where such legislation does not exist, offer protection to ethnic minorities and migrants. Moreover, international human rights standards and conventions oblige countries to adapt their national legislation and practices.
Special attention should be given to the Paris Charter for a New Europe (1990) signed by the then 29 CSCE Member States and to the UN Convention on the Elimination of all Forms of Racial Discrimination (1965). The Convention is signed by 129 states, but only 14 states have recognized the right of individual complaint.

Equality of treatment
Migrant workers, refugees and minorities must not only be

protected against racial discrimination but programmes should also be put in place that promote their full participation in society. Special attention should be given to the ILO Conventions relating to the position of legal and clandestine workers in the labour market, and the new UN Convention on the Protection of the Rights of all Migrant Workers and Members of their Families (1990).

Confronting root causes

NGOs can press for effective sanctions against undemocratic governments, for reducing international sale and trade of arms and for more equitable terms of trade and finance with less developed countries.

Notes

1. This article was originally presented as a paper for the international conference 'Human Rights of Migrant Workers. Agenda for NGOs.' (Manila, 19-20 November 1992), organized by the Scalabrini Migration Center, in co-operation with the ILO, the Friedrich Ebert Stiftung and Missio.
2. This part will mainly concentrate on Western Europe and only occasionally references are made to Eastern Europe.

Editorial note

The second volume of the series concerned will be entitled *Insiders and Outsiders*. Again this booklet will contain a wide variety of contributions. We are in touch with several authors who by now promised to supply an essay. E.g. Mary Grey (Britain) will deal with the theme 'Women and Europe', Herman Verbeek (MEP, Rainbow Group) will present an exposé on the farmer's unhappy lot in Europe and Wolfgang Huber is going to write on 'Germany and Europe'. Then we will also have at our disposal Bart Voorsluis' essay on 'The Identity of Europe: the ideas of Eugen Rosenstock-Huessy and Edgar Morin', which was not available because of the Amsterdam philosopher's health problems. Moreover, we intend to follow the tracks of the pattern present in the first volume, that is to say, the various contributions will highlight the problem from very different angles, a global-journalist, a feminist, an ethicist, a politician, a philosopher, etc.

From Horatio we received the old saying 'tua res agitur' – it is your concern. Yet Horatio added something: 'paries cum proximus ardet' – when your neighbour's house is on fire. Exactly for this reason we are all responsible for Europe, as if it is burning. Consequently, our discernment and commitment are involved.

Contributors

Ackermann, Bruno. Swiss national, completed his studies in literature and philosophy at the University of Lausanne. A Staff member of the Centre of European Culture at Geneva. He is preparing a doctoral dissertation on the spiritual legacy of De Rougemont.

De Lange, H.M. Trained as an economist, Dr. De Lange has published widely on ecumenical issues. Areas of interest include the Third World and an explicit option for the poor. His best-known book is *Rijke en Arme Landen* (1967). Now an emeritus-professor in Social Ethics at the University of Utrecht.

Forrester, Duncan B. Prof. Forrester teaches Christian Ethics and Practical Theology in the University of Edinburgh and is Principal of New College. Served from 1962-'70 as a missionary Professor teaching in Madras Christian College, and as a Presbyter of the Church of South India. His recent publications include *Beliefs, Values and Politics* (1990) and *Theology and Politics* (1989).

Hampson, Daphne. Beginning her career as a historian, Dr. Hampson wrote a doctoral thesis on the response in Brittain to the Church conflict in Germany during the Third Reich. This was followed by a Harvard doctorate in Systematic Theology. Since 1977 she has been a lecturer in Systematic Theology at the University of St.-Andrews. Recent publication: *Theology and Feminism* (1990).

Niessen, Jan. A Dutch sociologist who worked for more than ten years with associations of migrants and refugees, and was also involved in the Third World solidarity movement. At present he is General Secretary of the Churches Committee for Migrants in Europe (Brussels). Dr. Niessen has published many articles in newspapers and in scientific and other (inter)national magazines. He is also editor of the CCME Briefing Papers.

Ramonet, Ignacio. A journalist with *Le Monde Diplomatique*, a reputed French monthly involved in investigative jounalism in the field of politics, economics and culture.

Sedgwick, Peter. Dr. Sedgwick is lecturer in Theology at the University of Hull. Adviser in Industrial Issues to the Archbishop of York. Author of *Mission Impossible: a Theology of the Local Church* (1990) and *The Enterprise Culture* (1992).

Van Putten, Maartje. Prior to becoming a Member of the European Parliament (Socialist), Mrs. Van Putten was a journalist and staffed the Scientific Institute of the Dutch Labour Party. In the latter capacity and as a MEP her main area of interest is the Third World.

Wiersma, Alies. Attended the School of Art & Design in Enschedé (the Netherlands) and is at present involved in a project on *Art & Feminism* at Rotterdam.

Wiersma, Jurjen. Studied Theology in Amsterdam and Chicago. Prof. Wiersma teaches Ethics and Philosophy at the Faculty of Protestant Theology in Brussels. His inaugural lecture was entitled *Europe 1992 – Krisis of Kairos? Aspekten van een theologische probleemstelling* (1988).